Designing Schools for Meaningful

Professional Learning

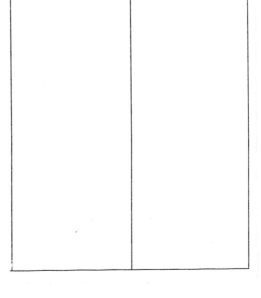

West Herts **College**

Learning Centres Service

WATFORD CAMPUS

HEMPSTEAD ROAD
WATFORD HERTS WD17 3EZ
TEL 01923 812554

4072862

Return on or before the last date stamped below.

Designing Schools for Meaningful Professional Learning

A Guidebook for Educators

Janice Bradley

Foreword by Shirley M. Hord

A Joint Publication

FOR INFORMATION:

Corwin

A SAGE Company

2455 Teller Road

Thousand Oaks, California 91320

(800) 233-9936

www.corwin.com

SAGE Publications Ltd.

1 Oliver's Yard

55 City Road

London EC1Y 1SP

United Kingdom

SAGE Publications India Pvt. Ltd.

B 1/I 1 Mohan Cooperative Industrial Area

Mathura Road, New Delhi 110 044

India

SAGE Publications Asia-Pacific Pte. Ltd.

3 Church Street

#10-04 Samsung Hub

Singapore 049483

Acquisitions Editor: Dan Alpert

Associate Editor: Kimberly Greenberg

Editorial Assistant: Cesar Reyes

Project Editor: Veronica Stapleton Hooper

Copy Editor: Matthew Connor Sullivan

Typesetter: C&M Digitals (P) Ltd.

Proofreader: Jeff Bryant

Indexer: Karen Wiley

Cover Designer: Scott Van Atta

Marketing Manager: Lisa Lysne

Printed in the United States of America

Cataloging-in-publication data are available for this title from the Library of Congress.

ISBN: 9781483339221

This book is printed on acid-free paper

SFI Certified Sourcing
www.sfiprogram.org
SFI-00453

14 15 16 17 18 10 9 8 7 6 5 4 3 2 1

Contents

Foreword

To *improve* anything—whether it is a garden for producing nutritious vegetables, or a means by which to develop students' understanding of latitude and longitude—non-effective factors or features must be deleted and *changed* to some having more potential for success; this change to the "new" requires *learning* what the change is and how to use it.

This means that adults in our schools, our educators, consistently undertake the improvement process of

- Reviewing a broad array of student performance data
- Identifying areas of students' low performance
- Specifying what is not working productively and adopting new practice that has the potential to generate more positive outcomes
- Learning what the adopted change is and how to effectively put it into classroom practice.

Adult learning in our schools is, thus, an imperative, and this professional learning must be continuous, of high quality, and designed with the most effective features possible so as to influence educators' new knowledge and skills that impact students' learning.

This is no small feat. But when new research and practice inform us of ways to conduct professional learning more effectively, it is essential to carefully consider how to insure that all adults' experience successful learning processes that will reach all classrooms, all schools, and all districts. The question demanding attention then is, How to move the successful model of the Five Part Plan (FPP), the focus of attention of the study reported in this book, across the landscape to all schools.

In summary, this Foreword provides a few <u>words</u> be<u>fore</u> the book begins and is cast in the understanding that

- any change (of knowledge, behaviors, skills, attitudes, etc.) requires relevant learning; and

- explicit learning can produce related changes in knowledge, behaviors, skills, attitudes, etc.

Professional learning and change process are therefore inextricably linked. This Foreword uses change process research to respond to the question above:

How to scale up the successful model of professional learning reported in this manuscript.

Because a foreword implies a short text, the suggestions and commentary provided here are done in a condensed and streamlined manner. Certainly, additional expository text and material are available through the references cited.

RESEARCH ON IMPLEMENTATION

After years of frustrations derived from the introduction of new practices, programs, and processes in schools failed to result in their quality use in classrooms across the US, the federal Department of Education requested a research team to identify the requirements that would move new practices into new classrooms. This team worked in multiple schools for multiple years to answer this question. The Concerns-Based Adoption Model (CBAM) (Hall & Hord, 2015; Hord & Roussin, 2013) was the result.

Tools for the Change Leaders/Facilitators

The findings from the research included the attention to creating tools whereby change leaders could gain awareness of potential and involved implementers' attitudes and reactions to new curriculum or new instructional protocols, for example (tool: Stages of Concern); implementers' behavioral approaches or how they were making the transition to using new programs (tool: Levels of Use); and, the progress made by implementers as they moved from novices who were initiating changes to experts in their use of innovations (tool: Innovation Configurations).

Strategies for Implementation

Importantly, this team also tracked the larger actions or long-term strategies that change leaders used to develop a game plan and its related actions for the introduction and complete transition of the change into appropriate classrooms, or other desired sites (Six Strategies: Moving from Adoption to Full Implementation). It is this larger framework to which attention is given in this short text (see Hord & Roussin, 2013; Hord, Rutherford, Huling, & Hall, 2014).

A FRAMEWORK OR GAME PLAN FOR IMPLEMENTATION

Any professional or arm-chair sports "expert," without question, will attest to the importance of the coaching team's plan for winning sports contests. Considering school improvement plans, there is no absolute certainty about the outcomes to be gained from any implementation plans. But, there is a large degree of confidence and success that can be derived from engaging the six strategies revealed in the research on implementation. For, it is implementation, or transfer of new practices to the sites where students may benefit from teachers' more effective teaching, that is the target of professional learning (Fullan, Hord, Von Frank, Chapter 2, 2014).

The initial step is to clarify the new practice, for all who will be involved—principals, teachers, teacher leaders, central office staff—whether they serve as implementers or facilitators of the change.

Articulate a Vision of the Change

One can easily think of implementation or the transfer of new practice into its desired sites as a journey. And, like any journey, the ultimate destination is required before one sets sail to initiate the journey to the end point. Thus, creating written text that defines and reflects the new practice *in operation* when it is fully implemented in a high quality way is the significant starting point of the change journey—we "begin with the end" (Lindsey, Lindsey, Hord, & Von Frank, Chapter 2, 2015).

Key words noted above are "in operation" for this text dictates what the desired results are in terms of action words, and active voice, that describe what each of the role groups involved (administrators, teachers, etc.) are doing, related to the new practices. This vision creation and articulation is the first strategy or step in the process of broadcasting any innovation (or new practice, program, process) to a larger setting.

A starting point is to analyze and specify the major components or parts of an innovation. In terms of the Five Part Plan (FPP), it appears that there are seven unique features that define the FPP. The first of these is the creation, by the school faculty, of an effective classroom-learning environment. Sharing the process and outcomes of the identification of five instructional practices that the entire school will pursue is a first part of the vision building. Who plays roles in this vision building? Most likely it is the principal, or possibly assistant principal. Or, it could be a strong teacher leader, or a district office person. Whoever the guide is, this person is joined by the teaching faculty, for this focus of the school's professional learning is made by the whole school. Other components of the FPP will need to be identified and clearly defined through action-oriented statements (see Innovation Configurations).

Invest in Professional Learning

Since the Bradley book is focused on the what, and the how that teaching staff are engaging in their learning, this strategy refers the reader to the book, for no foreword can do it justice. But, be sure to remember that successful adult learning that is transferred to classroom practice involves four steps (Joyce & Showers, 2002): (1) telling the educator learners about the new practice, (2) demonstrating or modeling it for the adult learners, (3) providing the learners with time for practice and giving feedback on the practices, (4) providing follow-up that includes facilitators who interact with the adult learners one-on-one to answer questions, clarify puzzlements, observe and elicit collaborative feedback based on the observations. Joyce and Showers research indicate that the first three steps are cumulative and that it is at the addition of the fourth step, follow up, that transfer is accomplished.

Construct an Implementation Plan and
Identify Required Resources

The FPP model of professional learning is a complex one involving not only knowledge and skills, but feelings of trust in oneself and in others, agreeable and positive relationship factors so that interaction within the teams is constructive, and learners' change, growth, and improvement occurs.

Time is a resource of enormous significance if this professional learning model is successful. In the book, the reader learns of the actions that principals took and the resources they accessed that supported the acquisition of necessary resources and the happy ending to this story of adult learning.

Needless to say, the FPP allows—demands—that teachers take on roles of deep study and exploration of instructional approaches and strategies, and further, that they make decisions unlike what they have been permitted to make in the past. There will, thus, be role changes, changes in allocations of budget items, possible changes in the school's schedules and other structural and relational conditions. This means that school personnel will take on new models of learning such as the FPP and they should be provided with explanations about the adjustments and re-alignment of schedules required for the changes inherent in the new professional learning model.

Assess Implementers' Growth and Progress

Despite implementers' provision of excellent professional learning processes and resources, time and much support are typically necessary for successfully transferring new programs and processes into new settings. To ensure that the support is truly helpful, assessing the degree to which implementers (in this case, the adults) are taking on new practices appropriately is critically important. The tools mentioned earlier in this manuscript can be used to do this assessing. The Innovation Configuration map is a tool created from the concept of multiple configurations of innovations and is a prime tool for assessing progress. For this clearly articulated text that describes the new practices in operation can be used as a measure to judge how close to "ideal" implementation is occurring.

Without this assessing, providing supportive assistance is impossible—to which we turn.

Provide Ongoing Assistance

As noted above, the idea is that Assessing and Assisting are like the proverbial hand in glove. This follow-up is what the research of Joyce and Showers cited; it is what the "one-legged conferences" of the CBAM are. This follow-up is the work that coaches typically do, to facilitate the implementation of new processes such as new professional learning models for the educators in schools.

In addition to using the data collected by observing implementers and their work, or by conducting short conversations to elicit "where she or he is" in gaining expertise with the new way," the facilitator who intends to support the implementer through helpful conversations and feedback, must develop a friendly, appreciative attitude, and respectful relationship with the implementer. Building trust is foundational.

Create a Context Supportive of Change

Working with an improvement-seeking faculty in a school or district makes change introduction relatively easy. When staff know that making a mistake when learning to use new schemes or processes will not result in flogging at high noon, this takes non-productive pressure off the implementing staff. Of course, mistakes are not invited, but in fact, they are used as opportunities for clarification and growth. Further, leaders of change who pay attention to the feelings and reactions of implementers (via Stages of Concern) by making adjustments based on SoC data go a long way toward creating a positive context that invites change . . . that will lead to improvement, that ultimately impacts students' successful learning.

ADOPTION

The six strategies that have been introduced briefly are used to construct plans for the implementation of new processes, such as the Five Part Plan, a new schema for providing professional learning in a school. There is, of course, a means by which to entice the innovative process to the school and/or district where it can be implemented. Broadcasting, communicating, or marketing the new process through articles in the educational journals and through presentation at educational conferences makes initial information available. This sequence of events precedes adoption and implementation and has its own challenges.

A major platform for introducing or adopting a new professional learning program or process rests on 1) enhancing the current process so that it is increasingly more effective, or 2) there is a critical *need* that is addressed by the new process. If there is not a need for a different way of providing and conducting professional learning, educators will likely be very reluctant to accept new professional learning practices. While current professional learning practices in many schools and in many districts are vital and enthusiastically engaged, there is the reality of dull and boring, off-target and totally ineffective professional learning that is being employed in many of our schools and districts. Consider this picture:

A presenter stands at a computer or other electronic device that advances slides. We hear click, click—lecture, lecture—click—lecture–click—lecture—- *ad nauseum.* The learner is not engaged, except to take notes perhaps, for what purpose? Is there a need for a new approach to professional learning here? You bet !

We know that effective learning that requires more than "cough back what you heard" must engage the learner, whether the learner is a young student or an adult educator. A significant way to engage adult learners is to provide them voice and choice in what they will learn and how to learn it—this theory has been richly manifested in the experiences reported in Bradley's book.

In addition to need, the wise school improver takes note of the environmental factors required for the success of a new process or program.

Bringing FPP to a school that is clearly unable to access the time and other resources necessary is a foolish enterprise.

Engaging an array of representatives of role groups to be involved in the study and exploration of a new professional learning process makes it possible to communicate effectively with all stakeholders. Informing stakeholders of the need, and the solution to address the need can be used to solicit their interest, approval and support in making the decision for adopting—bringing the new process to the school or district. Stakeholder reps can also aid in introducing the innovation, and doing so in the company of a make-it-yourself hot fudge sundae meeting might not be a bad idea.

The ideas shared in this Foreword come from research on school change, and from the experiences of practitioners in the field who employ the research and add to it. In this Foreword, the ideas are at the introduction level, and interested readers are invited to refer to the cited references for more information.

For certain, professional learning for our educators must be effective, and continuous. This thesis recently emerged in the comic pages of the daily news, where we see Dolly (of Family Circus, a pre-school or first grade pupil) being welcomed home after the first day of school by her mother who inquires, "Did you learn a lot on your first day?"

As she strolls away from her mother, Dolly replies, "Yes, but they want me to go back tomorrow anyway."

Indeed, we want our educators to go back tomorrow and the tomorrow after that, engaged in continuous professional learning such as the FPP model that invites them to participate in decision making, and results in becoming ever increasingly expert for teaching our students.

REFERENCES

Fullan, M., Hord, S. M. & Von Frank, 2014). *Reach the highest standard in professional learning: Implementation.* Thousand Oaks, CA: Corwin & Learning Forward.

Hall, G. E., & Hord, S. M. (2015). *Implementing change: Patterns, principles, and potholes* (4th ed.). Upper Saddle River, NJ: Pearson.

Hord, S. M., & Roussin, J. L. (2013). *Implementing change through learning: Concerns-based concepts, tools, and strategies for guiding change.* Thousand Oaks, CA: Corwin.

Hord, S. M., Rutherford, W. L., Huling, L., & Hall, G.E. (2014). *Taking charge of change.* Austin, TX: SEDL.

Joyce, B., & Showers, B. (2002). *Student achievement through staff development* (3rd ed.). Alexandria: VA: Association for Supervision and Curriculum Development.

Lindsey, D. B., Lindsey, R. B., Hord, S. M., & Von Frank, V. (2015). *Reaching the highest standard in professional learning: Outcomes.* Thousand Oaks, CA: Corwin & Learning Forward.

Shirley M. Hord, PhD
Scholar Laureate
Learning Forward
September 2014

Preface

Let's open a conversation space. Within these pages is a guidebook for how to design a school for meaningful professional learning using a supportive structure, called the Five-Part Plan (FPP). The FPP model provides teachers time and experiences to grow and advance into effective/highly effective facilitators of student learning through active engagement in self-selected learning designs. Unique features of the FPP include the following:

- Creating a shared vision among school staff for effective classroom learning environments
- Alignment to the teacher evaluation system
- Teachers self-selection of learning designs
- Opportunities for teachers to act as knowledge producers
- Attention to three dimensions of professional learning: technical, psychological/emotional, and social
- Knowledge Showcase
- Creation of a Professional Knowledge Base

For one year, the research-informed FPP was enacted at four schools—one high school and three elementary schools. It was created synergistically by principals, teacher leaders, and myself, the university partner, in response to a compelling need for teachers to have time to improve teaching practice as measured by teacher evaluation, and to create ownership in their learning. This book is meant to serve as a manual for educators who want to design schools for authentic, purposeful, and enjoyable professional learning. Strategies for implementation, along with stories of enactment and results, are included throughout the chapters.

FEATURES OF THE BOOK

Designing Schools for Meaningful Professional Learning explores how school-based educators can work collaboratively to create a highly effective, low-stress culture of collaboration and knowledge building for supporting student learning. Research, articles, and literature abound with theories and practices about effective professional learning, but it is often difficult for educators to find the planning time to translate theory into practice at their school. This book offers a detailed plan that responds to the need for teachers to find time to learn collaboratively through a variety of self-selected learning designs connected to their classroom and to advance teachers' facilitation of student learning as measured by the teacher evaluation system. Each chapter guides school-based educators with authentic highlights, successes, and challenges using comments and vignettes, and provides protocols, facilitation suggestions, and troubleshooting tips for implementation.

Chapter 1—Moving to Meaningful Professional Learning in Schools provides information from research and experts in the field about professional learning and what it currently looks like in schools. Decisions made about professional learning are examined, as well as who influences and makes those decisions. Reasons are explored for why schools should be intentionally designed for professional learning. The FPP for designing a school for meaningful professional learning is introduced in this chapter, accompanied by how the FPP aligns professional learning to teacher evaluation. Two unique ideas about professional learning are introduced in this chapter and explored in later chapters: (1) how teachers can become knowledge producers to inform and advance their practice, and (2) how teachers can create a Professional Knowledge Base for archiving successful practices in student learning.

Chapter 2—The Five-Part Plan: How to Design a School for Meaningful Professional Learning describes each part of the research-informed plan that four schools implemented for one year. Protocols and suggestions for facilitation are described in detail.

Part 1—Reaching Consensus results in the Five Agreements, a consensus among school staff about what five practices should be in every classroom every day to support student learning. Teacher evaluation elements align the Five Agreements with descriptors of effective/highly effective teaching methods to ensure the five practices are in concert with what will be measured.

Part 2—Selecting the Learning Design results in teachers selecting one of nine learning designs to learn how to become effective/highly effective with the Five Agreements.

Part 3—Implementing the Learning Design Cycle describes how teachers collaborate in two cycles of learning designs to connect learning outside of their classrooms to practice and enactment inside them.

Part 4—Sharing Professional Knowledge with Whole School Staff describes a Knowledge Showcase and how teachers share learning with evidence produced from participation in the two cycles of learning designs.

Part 5—Creating a Professional Knowledge Base illustrates how a school can archive knowledge so that successful strategies and practices are remembered.

Chapter 3—Cycles of Learning Designs Connected to the Classroom details nine learning designs supported by research and Learning Forward's Standards for Professional Learning. Each design consists of a protocol for enactment and is illustrated with a vignette from practice. In each protocol is a description of the design that includes studying and planning a classroom lesson with the new practice, enacting the lesson in the classroom collaboratively, and assessing student outcomes. Unique to the learning designs is nonjudgmental, descriptive feedback about student results and teaching outcomes apart from the teacher. The nine learning designs included in this chapter are the following: (1) Collaborative Teaching and Assessing, (2) Peer Teaching, (3) Vertical Team Study, (4) Intentional Practicing with Student Response, (5) Using Technology—Linked-In Lessons, (6) Studying Video and Application, (7) Lesson Study, (8) Shared Learning with Teachers, Principals, and Coaches, and (9) Creative and Innovative Teaching.

Chapter 4—The Power of Teachers Selecting Learning Designs explores the need to promote teacher self-efficacy through selection of learning designs, how and why teachers select specific designs, the benefits for teachers selecting learning designs, and ways in which the choice of learning designs connects to growth through teacher evaluation.

Chapter 5—Assessing and Evaluating Changes considers the difference between assessment and evaluation, and why assessment was an important term to use to determine the impact of the FPP. This chapter includes the results from implementing the FPP, specifically what was assessed and what improved as a result of teachers engaging in the FPP. A process to assess the FPP or any professional plan at a school is described, and a checklist is provided at the end of the chapter for a practitioner to use.

Chapter 6—The Principal: The Key to Making Learning Happen examines the crucial role of the principal in implementing the FPP, and the need for the principal to understand the value of professional learning to support and connect job-embedded learning to teacher evaluation. This chapter includes communication tools a principal can use to promote a climate of trust, and some "behind the scenes" actions a principal takes before introducing the FPP to staff.

Chapter 7—Three Dimensions of Learning Designs: Technical, Psychological/Emotional, and Social introduces three dimensions useful for developing and assessing learning designs: (1) Technical—how do you do it? (2) Psychological/Emotional—is it enjoyable for you? (3) Social—how do we learn together? Each dimension is explored through a research lens, and reasons are cited for why all three dimensions must be considered for professional learning to be an optimal experience.

Chapter 8—Building a School's Professional Knowledge Base proposes the development of a professional knowledge base and some reasons why each school should create one. Learning at three schools, from teachers' engagement in two cycles of learning designs, was scrutinized as to whether practices contributed to both teacher and student learning. Suggestions were made for knowledge that should be archived so as to allow ongoing access for other educators.

Chapter 9—Meaningful Learning to Remember synthesizes learning from implementation of the FPP during one school year. Addressed are the benefits and challenges, some final thoughts, and an invitation for all school-based educators to take creative action to design their schools for meaningful professional learning. Wise educators must respond to the need for teachers to have time and efficacy to engage in professional learning that leads to advances in student learning. When educators establish a climate of collaboration and a culture of continuous learning at a school, dramatic changes can happen.

Acknowledgments

Abundant gratitude and appreciation goes to the principals, teacher leaders, teachers, instructional coaches, and students who inspired the content of this guidebook. Without the cooperation and dedication of these amazing educators who took risks with me to grow and learn, this book would not exist. Special thanks goes to the talented and supportive professional educators who comprise the Mathematically Connected Communities (MC^2) and the MC^2–Leadership Institute for Teachers at New Mexico State University, who provided a collaborative, supportive place promoting growth and creative action, and to my husband, Steve, for his technical help, for taking time to listen and reflect, and for exhibiting great patience during the writing process.

PUBLISHER'S ACKNOWLEDGMENTS

Corwin gratefully acknowledges the contributions of the following reviewers:

Denny Berry
Assistant Professor (formerly Director, Cluster 6 Schools, Fairfax County Public Schools)
Curry School of Education, University of Virginia
Charlottesville, VA

Jenni Donohoo
Research Consultant
Greater Essex County District School Board
Windsor, ON

Bill Hall
Director of Educational Leadership & Professional Development
Brevard Public Schools
Viera, FL

Cate Hart Hyatt
Educational Consultant
Indiana University, Center on Education and Lifelong Learning
Bloomington, IN

Shirley M. Hord
Lecturer/Professional Developer, Independent Consultant—focus on school change/improvement, especially professional learning communities
Informal affiliation, Scholar Laureate, Learning Forward

Alysson Keelen
Howell Twp. Public School District
Adelphia School
Freehold, NJ

Nikki Golar Mouton
Executive Director of Staff Development
Gwinnett County Public Schools
Suwanee, GA

About the Author

 **Janice Bradley,** PhD, is a lifelong educator whose passion is to learn alongside educators to create equitable school cultures for powerful learning. She specializes in designing and facilitating authentic, relevant professional learning experiences for change and improvement in practice, with leaders at all levels of a school system, including leadership teams, principals, teacher leaders, instructional coaches, and mathematics teachers.

Bradley's classroom experience includes teaching at all elementary grade levels with students from diverse backgrounds. Her district-level experience was obtained through serving as a K–12 mathematics specialist and coordinating professional learning experiences for mathematics teachers and leaders.

At the university level, she has served as adjunct professor at three universities and currently is a faculty member at New Mexico State University. Her research interests include creating school climates for trust and collaboration, professional learning communities, systemic change, teacher leadership, and elementary mathematics.

At the national level, she served as a site coordinator on a collaborative project with SEDL and the Charles A. Dana Center, funded by the Department of Education, where she facilitated learning for systemic change with educators in six states. She facilitated learning sessions at numerous conferences, and served as a consultant for educators who want to integrate research into practice. Bradley holds a doctorate in mathematics education from the University of Texas at Austin. Her dissertation was on mathematics coaching.

Moving to Meaningful Professional Learning in Schools

1

"Professional learning can have a powerful effect on teacher skills and knowledge and on student learning if it is sustained over time."

—Linda Darling-Hammond (Hammond et al., 2009)

"Professional learning is about giving teachers the confidence to know they can be effective."

—Veronica, instructional coach

"The 'big picture' is designing a school so teachers have time for reflective practice and collaboration leading to improved instruction and improved student learning."

—Mashelle, high school assistant principal

In this chapter, the following questions are addressed:

- What is professional learning, and what does it look like in schools?
- Who is making decisions about professional learning, and what is being decided?
- Why should schools intentionally be designed for professional learning?
- What is the Five-Part Plan (FPP) for designing a school for meaningful professional learning?

- How can the FPP align professional learning to teacher evaluation?
- How can teachers become knowledge producers to create a Professional Knowledge Base (PKB)?

At the end of this chapter, you will be able to

- identify what is written about professional learning and how practices are enacted in schools;
- visualize who decides professional learning for teachers, and what content, type, and structures are decided;
- name ten reasons why schools should be intentionally designed for professional learning;
- develop awareness of the FPP and how it can be used to design schools for meaningful professional learning;
- identify how the FPP aligns professional learning to teacher evaluation; and
- consider teachers as knowledge producers who create a PKB.

Let's take a look into the lived experience of two sets of teachers as they begin their school year.

> **Vignette 1**: *During the last week in July, two experienced fourth-grade teachers, Heather and David, received a "Welcome Back to School" e-mail from the district's superintendent relaying information about the district's upcoming priority initiatives, along with dates for upcoming training sessions. The e-mail named the school district's newly adopted mathematics resource, along with information about the required one-day training given by its publisher. Also included was the schedule for the next day's training on the new teacher evaluation system in the morning, and the new short-cycle and state assessment systems in the afternoon.*
>
> *After the training sessions, teachers' comments revealed frustration. "It was all so fast, and I feel so overwhelmed! There are so many changes and so much new material to learn," complained Heather. "Yeah. Here we go again with everything new. I just wish we could find something solid that works and stick with it," added Enrique. "I'm nervous about the teacher evaluation system. It's going to be hard to get an effective rating. Every year, it's getting harder and harder to teach. When are we going to have the time to learn how to do all this stuff?"*

What kind of support would help Heather and Enrique overcome this sense of being overwhelmed and learn how to implement the new initiatives?

> **Vignette 2**: *Cathryn and Bernadette, first- and third-grade teacher leaders, respectively, met with their principal, Krista, and me in late May to discuss concerns for the next school year. Krista wanted to discuss what to do about "all the change and new information that's coming down the pike." She wanted to brainstorm ideas on how to*

support teachers to implement new initiatives. Because of this collaboration, a teacher-learning support structure emerged so teachers could not only learn the changes for the upcoming year, but also become part of the culture as an ongoing structure for teacher professional learning.

As expected, the teachers received their "Welcome Back" letter from the district in July. In the letter, they were notified about a new math textbook, changes in teacher evaluation, and the new short-cycle and state assessment systems. Fortunately, they already had a plan, so every teacher had time and opportunity to learn how to promote student achievement within in the context of the new teacher evaluations. Cathryn points out, "It's not going to be easy this year—there are so many new things." However, Bernadette adds, "We are ready. There's one hour each week for grade-level teams to meet to analyze data and plan. Then there's time for the professional Learning Design Cycles. We've got a support system in place."

Krista sums up that the plan is tied to our teacher evaluation, and teachers will have choices as to what they will learn, and how it will take place.

What was their plan, and how did they design their schools for ongoing, meaningful professional learning?

WHAT IS PROFESSIONAL LEARNING, AND WHAT DOES IT LOOK LIKE IN SCHOOLS?

Professional learning opportunities among school-based educators are very diverse. There exists a broad range in schools spanning from the highest quality of planned professional learning down to absolutely no opportunity for educators to grow and learn professionally.

What is known about professional learning at school sites, and how important is it for increasing student achievement? *Professional development* is defined as a comprehensive, sustained, and intensive approach to improving teachers' and principals' effectiveness in raising student achievement. It is "conducted among educators at the school and facilitated by well-prepared school principals and/or school-based professional development coaches, mentors, master teachers, or other teacher leaders" (Learning Forward, 2012). The *Standards for Professional Learning* outline "the characteristics of professional learning that lead to effective teaching practices, supportive leadership, and improved student results" (Learning Forward, 2012). Teachers learn collaboratively, with purpose, to improve their knowledge and skills resulting in high-quality support for all students' achievement.

When teachers engage in job-embedded professional development, they learn what practices increase student achievement. What does this actually look like in a school? How can this happen in a busy school today?

During a typical school year, where and how are teachers learning, when are they learning, what are they doing and learning, and how well are they learning?

Where and how are teachers learning?

Teachers may be sitting together in a room outside their classrooms, either in their professional learning communities (PLCs) or in collaborative learning teams that meet during school. They also may be learning together inside a classroom, sharing the implementation of a lesson designed together, or engaged in whole-faculty study.

You might see teachers "linked-in" to virtual learning networks or blogs, or watching videos modeling formative assessment strategies. There may or may not be a system in place to support teachers to ensure transfer of learning (Joyce & Showers, 2002).

When are teachers learning?

One vision is that teachers learn organically, and seamlessly, every day. As a teacher, you would consistently hear and participate in conversations rich with ways to support students. Realistically, what you see are teachers choosing to meet for thirty minutes to one hour at weekly or biweekly intervals during the school day. An alternative to this may include professional development sessions held during half-day early release days. On the other hand, perhaps it is more convenient after school or on a designated day without students, either before school starts or during the school year.

What are teachers doing and learning?

Teachers may be looking at student work to assess understanding of standards, designing a lesson that increases students' engagement, or studying formative assessment practices to elicit student understanding of content and process. In some cases, teachers are asked to learn the new curriculum, analyze data, learn the new assessment system, better understand the new teacher evaluation system, or learn new security procedures. The content of what teachers learn may or may not be intentionally or directly related to improving teacher effectiveness or connected to student learning. The content may be about managing and better understanding state mandates and organizational functioning, or analyzing data from a continuous improvement cycle.

How well are teachers learning?

A monitoring system may or may not be in place. If professional learning is evaluated for impact, multiple data sources are used, which may include teacher and student reflections, interviews, and teacher evaluation observations correlated to student scores. If a monitoring system is nonexistent, there will be no indicators of the impact of teacher learning.

What is actually happening with professional learning in schools?

What follows is a look into six schools, which either already have or do not have ongoing professional learning as formally defined. What are the different enactments of professional learning at these schools? After reading the descriptions, can you guess which schools are intentionally designed for professional learning that is meaningful for teachers and will result in gains in student achievement?

School A—High School. All departments meet weekly. The math department at this high school is led by a strong department chair. The chair organizes, plans, and facilitates weekly one-hour meetings with seven math teachers. The content of the meetings is determined by the chair, who spends time before the meeting soliciting teacher input into relevant issues for discussion. Data from benchmark assessments, short-cycle student assessments, and test scores are used at each meeting to make instructional decisions and determine intervention supports for students. The principal asks that the math department keep records of their meetings to document the team's learning over time. The principal attends ten minutes of a meeting at least once a month to show support and interest for the teachers' learning. Math teachers also participate in the FPP for professional learning (see Chapter 2), and engage in a minimum of two cycles per school year of their chosen professional learning design. The department chair states,

> The purpose of our work is to collaborate and learn together. To study something together and try it in a classroom setting, reflect, and share learning with one another and contribute to a professional learning knowledge base. Our professional learning model provides documentation for Domain 4 ["Professionalism" development domain on the state teacher evaluation] for participating in a PLC and providing learning and leadership opportunities for teachers.

School B—High School. The math department meets monthly after school to discuss testing, pacing, and student passing and failure rates, and to hear schoolwide organizational announcements. The department chair plans and facilitates each meeting. The principal requires department meetings and rarely attends meetings unless there is a problem or last-minute announcement. Teachers have not been required to attend district-level professional development trainings off campus in the last ten years. The district experienced an economic shortfall and has had no money to provide professional development sessions or send teachers to conferences. One teacher states, "I would like to learn more. We do not have the time or money."

School C—Middle School. All teachers are required to attend department meetings twice per month during the hours of 8:00 am to 8:20 am. The instructional coach is "in charge" of all meetings, meaning that he sets the agenda without input from other teachers, identifies topics for discussion, and directs all meetings. The principal attends the first part of the meeting on average once per month to give teachers announcements that he says are "important and timely information." At one meeting, the principal "took over" and used fifteen of the twenty minutes allotted for the meeting to emphasize his points and share district information about using short-cycle assessment data effectively. The instructional coach did not have an opportunity to share several planned agenda items. Every year, teachers attend three days of professional development outside the classroom chosen by district-level administrators. There is no input from teachers as to the nature of the training. One teacher states, "We just go through the motions and do what we are told."

School D—Middle School. All teachers meet weekly in PLCs by course (language arts, social studies, math, etc.) for fifty-five minutes. At the beginning of the school year before students arrived, the whole school staff studied PLCs to understand the "nuts and bolts." This included how to start a PLC, facilitate the meetings, deal with conflict, set norms, track learning, use data, and decide on content to talk about during the meeting time. By the end of the year, four out of six teams were operating as a PLC as measured on a rubric with five indicators (Hord, Roussin, & Sommers, 2010):

- Shared values and vision
- Collective responsibility
- Reflective professional inquiry
- Collaboration
- Individual and group learning

The principal checked in with the whole school staff in January to assess successes and challenges with learning in a PLC and attended each PLC meeting for at least five minutes once per month. PLC time was not used for management and sharing organizational information. Teachers regularly used data to drill down to student needs and decide what teachers needed to learn to improve student performance. During one nine-week grading period, the math PLC collected data from students and teachers about their perceptions of teaching and learning. Every week, the students and teachers rated the same five indicators, and this continuous feedback greatly helped to illuminate which teaching methods made students feel successful. For example, one student said, "Learning targets helped me know what the lesson was about," and another commented, "My teacher listened and valued my opinion." Teachers analyzed the data and compared their perceptions with those of students. The results revealed that there was often a discrepancy between the teacher and student perceptions. Teachers frequently rated themselves differently than their students rated them. The data helped teachers align behaviors and instructional actions to better support students. As one teacher in this PLC commented, "We work and learn well as a team. We've learned what students need and how we can change to support them."

School E—Elementary. Teachers in this school have no time to meet collaboratively during the school day, but the district allocates six early release days per year for district-level planned professional development. Teachers attend compliantly or "get written up" for not attending. What teachers learn during the six days may or may not be directly related to their own or their students' needs. A group of district-level administrators and instructional coaches make decisions about the content of the professional development based on their perceptions of teachers' needs, such as information on the state teacher evaluation system, how to use the new curriculum resources, and how to use the short-cycle assessment system. Teachers learned in August that their short-cycle assessment data would be factored into their final teacher evaluation score, and that they "should study the short cycle 'red zones'"—the places where students score the lowest—and provide extra support during the school day. Teachers leave the sessions with more questions than answers. According to the state standards, students are supposed to master certain concepts and skills by the end of the year. How can students be expected to score proficiently on assessment items that they have not yet learned? One teacher asked, "What am I supposed to pay attention to—the short-cycle data that effects my teacher evaluation, the state standards, or what the textbook says?"

School F—Elementary. Teachers in this school have a supportive principal who, with the help of teacher leaders at each grade level and the instructional coach, designed the school for professional learning by putting two structures in place.

<u>Structure 1:</u> Grade-level collaborative teams meet weekly for fifty minutes to study data and individual students, and suggest ways to intervene and support student needs.

<u>Structure 2:</u> The FPP for professional learning (see Chapter 2) where teachers choose a learning design based on their specific interests and learning needs, and engage in at least two cycles of the design using the three-part cycle—plan, teach, and assess/reflect.

At this school, teachers' attitudes about professional learning are positive. The instructional coach states,

> Teachers are very excited at the results they are getting and continue to get in their math lessons. This strategy comes in handy in third grade with the multiplication unit. Teachers continue to use this method with story problems and have found it very useful in students' explanations of their answers. We began this semester with a new learning design focused on reading. Teachers loved the video lesson design so much and found it very powerful to see the strategies in action that we are continuing to use it. Our focus is on discourse and close reading.

Did you recognize which schools are and are not intentionally designed for supporting teachers' professional learning? Can you predict which schools are and are not showing gains in student achievement? At which schools do you think teachers find their professional learning meaningful, that is, having an important quality and purpose?

WHO IS MAKING DECISIONS ABOUT PROFESSIONAL LEARNING, AND WHAT IS BEING DECIDED?

The goal is to support teachers in improving professional practices through active engagement in meaningful learning activities. Educators who decide the type, content, and structure for teachers' professional learning are typically people other than classroom teachers, such as district-level administrators (assistant superintendent, director of curriculum and instruction, professional development director, or coordinator), principals, and instructional coaches. Administrators base decisions on a variety of factors, which include what teachers need to know about new initiatives, state mandates, new and existing district policies, and availability of resources for professional learning, including time and money. Classroom teachers are typically not asked to give input toward making decisions about their own professional learning. Current research indicates that teachers in high-performing countries have involvement in decision making about their own professional learning (Darling-Hammond, Wei, Andree, Richardson, & Orphanos, 2009, p. 26). Some states are moving to using individual learning plans for teachers to align professional learning to their needs as determined by teacher evaluation observations and student test scores. Teachers get to choose from a menu of activities, including online modules, webinars, and videos, to increase knowledge and skills for effective student learning.

Teachers' written reflections and interviews show they would like to have input into choosing experiences that are relevant and meaningful for addressing their students' needs. Teachers want to engage in professional learning experiences focused on the content they teach, classroom management, and teaching special needs students. When teachers engage in training on topics that are chosen for them, these are often perceived as lacking purpose, relevance, and meaning. It begs the question for district administrators who choose professional learning for teachers: Are the professional learning experiences we are funding with scarce resources (consultant fees, costs for substitute teachers, teacher stipends, etc.) really supporting teacher learning in the most efficient and effective way? Without engaging the teachers first in the formation of their own professional learning, we may be missing a great opportunity to engage teachers in meaningful professional learning.

Sometimes bad timing adds to teachers' sense of disenfranchisement, even if they have the desire to learn. Here's an example: A principal of an elementary school scheduled math consultants to spend three hours with every grade level in their school building over three days. Teachers were scheduled to meet with the consultants to plan a lesson collaboratively, enact the lesson in the classroom with all teachers observing, then reflect and assess student understanding as a result of participating in the lesson. Substitutes were placed in classrooms and rotated every three hours so teachers could participate in the lesson design and implementation. When the kindergarten and first-grade teams arrived at 8:30 am, teachers were disgruntled and aggravated. One teacher commented,

> It's not that I don't want to be here. I just wish someone would ask me if this was a good day and time to work with consultants. This week I have report cards due, individual testing for all the students, and parent teacher conferences. Three hours out of the class is taxing! I feel so overwhelmed.

Needless to say, it took about ten minutes for teachers to vent before engaging fully in the learning. Teachers wish to be asked and included in scheduling professional learning, otherwise they feel that any professional learning experience decided by others is "done to them."

Let's look again at Schools A through F, the schools introduced earlier in this chapter. Who decides the content and type of professional learning for the teachers at these schools, and what data is used to decide?

Table 1.1 Who Decides Professional Learning? How Is It Decided?

School	Who decides the professional learning?	How is it decided?
School A—High School	Teachers, department chair, principals, instructional coach, external and partner consultants	Student test data, short-cycle assessments, teacher requests and input, external partnerships, such as High Schools That Work
School B—High School	District-level administrators (directors of curriculum and instruction and of professional development, instructional coaches)	Availability of funding from district
School C—Middle School	District-level administrators (assistant superintendent, directors of curriculum and instruction and of professional development), principals, instructional coaches, external and partner consultants	Current district initiatives, availability of funding, school-based initiatives, participation in partnerships
School D—Middle School	Principals, instructional coach, teachers, students	Data from state tests and short-cycle assessments, teacher requests and input, teacher evaluation data, student perceptual data
School E—Elementary School	District-level administrators (directors of curriculum and instruction and of professional development), instructional coaches	Availability of funding, current district initiatives
School F—Elementary School	Principals, instructional coach, teachers	Data from state tests, short-cycle assessments, teacher evaluation, teacher requests

Notice that Schools A, D, and F use multiple data sources to assess teachers' and students' learning needs, and request teachers' input in informing the content, type, and design for their own professional learning. *Schools A, D, and F also happen to be the schools where student achievement is increasing.*

WHY SHOULD SCHOOLS INTENTIONALLY BE DESIGNED FOR PROFESSIONAL LEARNING?

Research, knowledge, and experience provide compelling reasons for designing schools for professional learning (Borko, 2004; Darling-Hammond, 2009; Garet, Porter, Desimone, Birman, & Yoon 2001; Guskey, 2002, Learning Forward, 2012). The evidence is so compelling that one might wonder if there is any justifiable reason not to learn how to design schools for effective professional learning.

Here are ten compelling reasons:

1. Correlates to student achievement gains. According to the key findings from research about professional learning, countries that outperform the U.S. on international assessments spend a larger percentage of allocated funds per pupil on professional learning for teachers (Darling-Hammond, 2009).

2. Provides support for new teachers. The rapid soaring of the teaching force has resulted in an outpouring of beginning teachers, which includes young teachers and a growing number of older people switching careers. In 2003–2004, 68% of public school teachers with fewer than five years of experience participated in a new teacher induction program during the first year of teaching. By 2007–2008, the modal teacher was not a fifteen-plus-year veteran but a beginner in his or her first year of teaching (Ingersoll & Merrill, 2010).

3. Provides ongoing learning connected to practice. Teachers do not have to leave their school buildings to drive across town or long distances if they live in a rural community. Teachers use the classroom as the source and context for teaching and learning (Darling-Hammond, 2009).

4. Focuses on the teaching and learning of specific academic content. Teachers report that they rarely have time to talk about or increase their content knowledge for the subject area they teach. This is especially relevant to elementary teachers who teach math and science.

5. Builds strong working relationships with teachers at and across grade levels. Teachers sometimes have an opportunity to learn with partner grade-level teachers if they have time to collaborate built into their schedule, but only rarely have an opportunity to learn with a teacher from another department or grade level.

6. Provides useful learning opportunities. The low ratings by U.S. teachers of the usefulness of most professional development activities are indicators of the insufficiency of the professional development infrastructure now in place in most states and communities. Their top priorities are learning more about the content they teach (23%), classroom management (18%), teaching students with special needs (15%), and using technology in the classroom (14%). Almost half of American teachers indicate that most of their professional learning is not useful or valuable. However, most teachers (59%) say that content-related professional learning is useful (Darling-Hammond, 2009).

7. Strengthens teaching and learning for supporting English-language learners (ELL) and teaching special education students. More than 66% of teachers nationally have not received any learning experiences for supporting the learning of ELL or special education students. When professional learning is situated at the school site and in the classroom, it gives teachers an opportunity to learn how to support and focus on specific needs of their students—not other teachers' students (Darling-Hammond, 2009).

8. Provides time for teachers to collaborate and learn together in the classroom. Teachers in high performing countries have more time for professional learning. Schools are designed to give teachers time to participate in opportunities to improve practice. To reiterate, nations that outperform the United States on international assessments provide time for collaboration in teachers' regular work hours.

9. Provides teachers opportunities to participate in extended learning experiences and productive collaborative communities. These opportunities include working together on planning lessons using effective instructional strategies, learn from peer teaching and mentoring, conduct action research, and collaboratively assess student thinking, understanding, and performance, then identify appropriate academic interventions to support the students' progress.

10. Provides teachers voice and influence in crucial areas of decision making. When teachers have voice in choosing their professional learning, they find the learning relevant and meaningful, which can contribute to their overall effectiveness. In high-achieving countries, teachers have significant influence on decisions related to curriculum, assessment, and the design of their own professional learning. Currently in the United States, less than one-fourth of teachers feel they have any influence over their own professional learning, or decisions related to what they teach, how they teach, or how they assess student learning (Darling-Hammond, 2009).

> When schools are intentionally designed for professional learning, it means that time, resources, and structures have been put in place for comprehensive, sustained, and intensive approaches to improving teachers' and principals' effectiveness in raising student achievement. The principal clearly communicates expectations for teacher participation. Teachers have a voice in shaping the professional learning. Research strongly suggests schools must be strategically designed so that their staffs will realize the vision for professional learning that "every educator engages in effective professional learning every day so every student achieves" (Learning Forward, 2012). Overwhelming initiatives—teacher evaluation, state assessments, and whatever program the district has bought into—present a challenge for educators to find time and space to engage in professional learning. The FPP, used to design learning in four schools (see Chapter 2), can create a new learning ecology to foster and promote among the teachers a sense of belonging, ownership, trust, and support—all of which are essential for effective learning. The FPP can help turn schools into organic knowledge organizations with teachers as knowledge producers that encourage a high degree of creativity, adaptability, and emergent collaboration (Gloor, 2006; Scardemalia & Bereiter, 2006).

WHAT IS THE FIVE-PART PLAN FOR DESIGNING A SCHOOL FOR MEANINGFUL PROFESSIONAL LEARNING?

The FPP is a doable, manageable strategy for designing a school to ensure that teachers have opportunities to engage in effective professional learning connected to their classrooms, empowers teachers to select learning designs based on relevance to their needs, and links job-embedded learning to the teacher evaluation system. The FPP resulted from conversations with principals and teacher leaders about how teacher growth could be supported in first-year implementation of the state's new teacher evaluation system. Drawing from research and articles on professional learning, an action plan was developed to transfer research into practice. When I first e-mailed the plan to Krista, an elementary principal, she responded, "This is just what I needed! Something doable so we don't fall into the trap of 'not enough time' and an 'inch deep—mile wide.'" When Maria, an elementary principal, first heard about the plan, she stated, "This plan ties perfectly to the state teacher evaluation and draws on teachers' innate passions, abilities, and beliefs." Brandee, elementary instructional coach, shared the plan with Ray, principal, and both expressed the belief that the plan would support teacher growth with teacher evaluation. Mashelle, the high school assistant principal, stated that the "plan coincides with 'High Schools That Work' key practices, complements the new teacher evaluation system supporting Domains 1, 2, 3, and 4, and provides support for math teachers in 'hands-on' learning the new system."

The FPP comprises the following:

Part 1—Reaching Consensus

What five things should be in every classroom every day?

Part 2—Selecting the Learning Design

How do teachers learn to do those five things effectively?

Part 3—Implementing the Learning Design Cycle

What is a Learning Design Cycle, and how is it implemented?

Part 4—Sharing Professional Knowledge with Whole School Staff

What is a "Knowledge Showcase"?

Part 5—Creating a Professional Knowledge Base

How does a school archive learning so it is not lost?

Strategies and procedures for implementing the FPP are detailed in Chapter 2.

HOW CAN THE FIVE-PART PLAN ALIGN PROFESSIONAL LEARNING TO TEACHER EVALUATION?

How can a school's professional learning design connect to teacher evaluation?

The adoption of the Common Core State Standards (CCSS) by the vast majority of states, and new state standards in the other states, creates a pressing need to "do things differently," to accomplish the goals of the new program. The overarching vision for using CCSS and other standards leads to students being college and career ready, but to achieve these results, educators will need to identify and make appropriate changes in what and how students learn and then accurately measure student understanding.

To realize these changes, most states have designed teacher evaluation systems to encourage and document teacher growth. The Framework for Teaching (Danielson, 2013) serves as a research base for state-level teacher evaluation instruments. Underlying the research is the notion that students learn when cognitively engaged at high levels. According to Danielson, the procedures needed to evaluate teachers must be ones that can impact teacher learning. Effecting these changes (to increase levels of student engagement) requires that teachers must have opportunities to engage in necessary, relevant, and meaningful professional learning.

Images From Schools

Let's look at how two schools connect or do not connect professional learning to teacher evaluation:

School F—Professional Learning Connected to Teacher Evaluation

Summary of Process
Whole school staff, supported by a culture of curiosity and growth,

- reached consensus on five practices should be in every classroom every day;
- engaged in dialogue about effective teaching resulting in student learning;
- aligned the five practices with the teacher evaluation rubric;
- connected teacher evaluation domain elements to effective teaching; and
- chose professional learning designs to become effective as measured by the teacher evaluation domains.

Principal, teachers, and instructional coach created ownership and support for using teacher evaluation productively and aligned professional learning experiences to teacher evaluation domain elements.

School F's principal created a dialogue with whole school's staff about what constitutes effective/highly effective teaching to develop a shared understanding of quality practice. Before school started, teachers engaged in a study of research and articles on what counts as evidence of good teaching. The principal, with the help of a teacher leader group and instructional coach, set out to create a culture of continuous learning, professional curiosity, and inquiry. The staff looked at Domains 1 through 4 of the state's new teacher evaluation framework (Planning and Preparation, Classroom Environment, Instruction, Professionalism) and correlated the elements of each domain to their vision. The principal asked, "How can each of us learn how to be effective/highly effective at each element?" This principal then guided the staff through the FPP for designing their year for professional learning (see Chapter 2). Teachers chose professional learning experiences and designs based on the domain elements that needed strengthening. Along with the principal's leadership and use of the FPP, the teachers saw the connections between their vision of effective teaching, the teacher evaluation instrument, and the type of professional learning needed to be an effective teacher. At the end of the session, one teacher remarked, "I feel supported. I'm so glad my principal 'gets it' and gives us time to learn together with these learning designs." Written and verbal reflections indicated that the majority of the staff found the process purposeful and meaningful.

School C—Professional Learning Not Connected to Teacher Evaluation

Summary of Process

- Principal introduced the teacher evaluation instrument to all teachers.
- Staff studied each domain to understand what was expected of each teacher.
- Principal shared that few teachers would score effective and even fewer highly effective.
- Principal discussed schedule for observations.

School C's principal announced to his faculty on the first day of the start of a new school year that the state adopted a new teacher evaluation system, and that "you will get to study it today to learn what is expected of you." The teacher evaluation packets were then distributed to each teacher along with study guides for each of the four domains. Teachers spent the next five hours studying the domains and elements, and the descriptors for ratings for each element. The principal announced that few teachers will score effective, and even fewer will be highly effective. He suggested that teachers spend personal time studying the domain elements or use some of their twenty-minute team time weekly to learn what it takes to be effective. The principal concluded the session by commenting that doing all the observations will be difficult for him. He then shared a possible schedule of observations for teachers, and said that he expected full cooperation from everyone. At the end of the day, one teacher said, "This feels like a 'gotcha.' It seems impossible to be effective. I feel judged and graded with no support on how to get better."

HOW CAN TEACHERS BECOME KNOWLEDGE PRODUCERS TO CREATE A PROFESSIONAL KNOWLEDGE BASE?

At the beginning of each school year, educators at all levels of a school system—teachers, principals, instructional coaches, district administrators—set forth on a journey toward improving classroom teaching to provide students with opportunities for academic success. To improve teaching effectiveness so every student has a chance for success, the professional must have a knowledge base that improves over time so teachers know what practices work and should continue to be used, or do not work and should be abandoned from daily practice (Hiebert, Gallimore, & Stigler, 2002). How do teachers perceive knowledge development? Rather than perceive themselves as knowledge consumers or knowledge transmitters, what would happen if teachers perceived themselves as knowledge builders and their school as a knowledge-creating culture? Knowledge of effective instruction, use of data, and assessment could advance as a community so teachers have knowledge *of* instead of knowledge *about* (Scardamalia & Bereiter, 2006). See Chapter 8 for elaboration on the idea of teachers as knowledge producers and how the shift in perception could improve practice.

What knowledge do teachers produce to improve their practice? How do teachers know what methods, strategies, and approaches either do or do not promote student achievement? Do teachers and their systems learn from the past? Let's take a look at School B, a school that was given a grade of "D" from the state reporting system that measures school performance. For the last five years, student achievement scores continually decreased. The average number of students passing state math tests is 32%. Dropout rates are at an all-time high, 38%, and teacher morale is low. Some label this school as "toxic" and "dysfunctional." The "blame game" is alive and well at School B. Teachers blame the district for not choosing effective curriculum resources, and students for being lazy. The principal blames the teachers for their unwillingness to change and lack of support from the district to dismiss ineffective teachers. The district complains about the performance and has changed principals twice in five years, hoping that the situation improves. In math classrooms, for example, a teacher explains methods for doing a math worksheet correctly, students are listening, then working alone quietly from a textbook. Student participation was not encouraged. In other classrooms, teachers were doing most of the talking. Student engagement was "ineffective" as measured by the teacher evaluation instrument. Are current practices ones that contribute to student learning in the twenty-first century? Do the teachers and students at this school know what practices contribute to students' continual low performance, or are they aware of practices they could change to increase student achievement?

Let's move from this dismal picture to what a PKB could do to help this school.

Just imagine . . .

A whole school staff meets for one day, uses data to identify that student engagement is low, reads research on effective instructional practices that engage students at high levels, then chooses five practices to learn more about and how to apply in the classroom. Finally, the teachers agree to implement at least one practice per month during lessons and reflect on the results at weekly team meetings. What if teachers collected data from students on how well they were engaged during the practice? Would anything change? And what if teachers kept an online folder of "Increasing Student Engagement" strategies and also kept a short record of the five strategies they tried with results, and identified strategies to keep in the folder or delete from practice? Teachers at this school would now be building a PKB of practices they tried with evidence of results, and know that they—the teachers—were the knowledge producers that created the changes. See Chapter 9 for examples of the PKBs created by teachers based on their one-year implementation of the FPP for professional learning.

YOUR TURN—START THE CONVERSATION

Choose one or more of the questions that seem relevant to professional learning at your school or district and start the conversation!

- How do the teachers, principals, and coaches define professional learning in your school?
- How is your school designed for professional learning?
- When do teachers learn, where and how do they learn, and what do they talk about and do when they meet?
- Who designs professional learning in your schools, and how is the type, content, and structure decided?
- How is professional learning meaningful for teachers?

- How is teacher professional learning connected to teacher evaluation?
- How do current professional learning experiences build teachers' knowledge and skills for scoring effective or highly effective on teacher evaluation instruments?
- What input do teachers have in making decisions about professional learning? How do teachers have a voice in deciding their own professional learning?
- Do teachers perceive themselves as knowledge producers or knowledge consumers?
- Does your school build a PKB? If yes, what does it look like? If no, what would happen if learning was archived and built on each year?
- How do current professional learning experiences build teachers' knowledge and skills for scoring effective or highly effective on teacher evaluation instruments?
- If the intention of professional learning is to improve teachers' and principals' effectiveness in raising student achievement, then how can data from the teacher evaluation instruments be used to design professional learning?

The Five-Part Plan 2

How to Design a School for Meaningful Professional Learning

"The [Five-Part Plan (FPP)] gave me a real framework to put into place what will work with many different professional development endeavors. Any topic can be addressed through the Five-Part Plan. Teachers have choices as to what and how their learning takes place."

—Krista, elementary principal

"The FPP is about giving teachers the time to build confidence and skills to know that they can be effective."

—Veronica, instructional coach

"The FPP gave us a chance to work together and talk about vertical pieces—expectations, strategies, implementation, student performance, how to look at what English-language learner students will need to be successful in a dual language program."

—Cathryn, first-grade teacher

In this chapter, the following questions are addressed:

- How do you design a workplace that promotes and enhances professional learning?
- What is the Five-Part Plan (FPP), and how is it implemented?

- What is the timeline for implementing the FPP?
- What does the FPP look like in practice?
- What is your school's capacity for implementing the FPP?

At the end of this chapter, you will be able to

- identify a way to design your school for promoting meaningful professional learning;
- understand and know how to implement the FPP;
- know how to create a timeline and schedule for implementation; and
- identify your school's readiness capacity for implementing the plan.

HOW DO YOU DESIGN WORKPLACES THAT PROMOTE AND ENHANCE PROFESSIONAL LEARNING?

When educators start the new school year, there are predictable rhythms and activities. Let's look at the start of the school year at Status Quo Elementary. Two weeks prior to when staff returns, the principal attends district trainings and learns about the latest initiatives. Following the meeting, the principal and assistant principal, or the instructional coach, plan activities for one day of school-based *staff development*—the term most often used by teachers to describe any time they are not in their classroom getting ready for the first day of school. Teachers at Status Quo are not involved in planning or facilitating the day's outcomes and activities. On the first day back after summer break, the staff meets together for conversation accompanied by coffee, juice, and fruit. The formal meeting begins with the principal sharing the year's latest district initiatives and mandates with the whole staff. Included in the agenda is the new teacher evaluation system and changes in statewide assessments. Teachers also hear the "good or bad" news about their school's assessment data and report card grade from the previous year. Following the "data news," there is either a public celebration, lots of clapping and cheering for increased student scores and school report card grades, or sadness and frustration expressed by silence or moans for decreased scores and grades. The whole school staff, led by the principal, sets a new course of action for how the upcoming school year can be better than the one before. The meeting can end with teachers either being excited about starting the new school year or mentally buried in an avalanche of overwhelm.

Let's create a new beginning to the school year by sharing Terra Elementary School's process. Imagine a team of educators composed of a principal, instructional coach, and two teacher leaders sitting around a table in May. They are there to design their school year to include intentional, job-embedded professional learning connected to their classrooms. The team proposes that teachers choose their own professional learning areas based on student and teacher needs that will provide direction for teachers' learning throughout the year. The principal expresses interest, seems encouraged, and wants additional details. After several conversations, the group of educators consults with a university partner, and the FPP for professional learning emerges. The plan is designed to result in five primary outcomes:

1. Shared vision by all staff members for highly effective teaching and learning connected to teacher evaluation

2. Teacher choice of professional learning designs

3. Collaborative application and practice of new learning in the classroom

4. Public sharing of professional knowledge produced from participation in learning designs

5. Development of a Professional Knowledge Base (PKB)

Unique features of the FPP include teacher voice in planning and facilitating the five-part sessions, whole school focus, and consensus on what practices should be in every classroom, every day. Teacher choice of professional learning designs is the cornerstone for creating a learning environment where students succeed.

On the first day back from summer break, the principal at Terra shares the good news that the school's assessment data and report card grade improved. Predictable cheers and hurrahs erupted followed by the principal stating,

> We can't stop here. We have to keep learning and all move toward being effective and beyond. In order to do that, we must get on the same page with what practices should be in every classroom every day, and find time to learn how to become highly effective at those things.

The principal, two teacher leaders, and the university partner proceed to facilitate Parts 1 and 2 of the FPP to design their school for year-round professional learning.

WHAT IS THE FIVE-PART PLAN, AND HOW IS IT IMPLEMENTED?

The FPP is a research-informed model used to design the school year for teachers to have opportunity to actively engage in self-selected learning designs connected to the classroom. The FPP aligns professional learning opportunities for teachers to grow and improve effectiveness to the state teacher evaluation system. Unique to the FPP is the attention to three dimensions for professional learning: technical, psychological/emotional, and social (see Chapter 7). The five parts of the model include (1) creating a shared vision among whole school staff for highly effective classroom learning environments, (2) selecting research-based learning designs, (3) actively engaging collaboratively in two cycles of the chosen learning design, (4) sharing learning at a Knowledge Showcase at the end of the school year, and (5) documenting and archiving the learning in a PKB. The FPP was implemented at four schools, one high school and three elementary schools, for one year. Stories of enactment and results are included throughout the book, especially in Chapters 5 and 9. The following section provides a description and protocols for implementation.

The FPP for Designing Your School for Professional Learning

Part 1—Reaching Consensus

What five things should be in every classroom every day?

Part 2—Selecting the Learning Design

How do teachers learn to do those five things effectively?

Figure 2.1 Five-Part Plan (FPP) Timeline

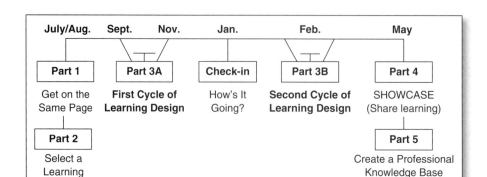

Part 3—Implementing the Learning Design Cycle

What is a Learning Design Cycle, and how is it implemented?

Part 4—Sharing Professional Knowledge with Whole School Staff

What is a "Knowledge Showcase"?

Part 5—Creating a Professional Knowledge Base

How does a school archive learning so it is not lost?

Part 1—Reaching Consensus

The purpose of "reaching consensus" is for all school-based educators to share the same vision about classroom learning environments before students arrive.

- What teacher and student practices, actions, and behaviors should occur in every classroom, every day to support student learning?
- What would happen if every teacher, instructional coach, and principal at the same school agreed on five things—practices, behaviors, and actions—that should be in every classroom every day to support student learning?
- How do educator beliefs align with domain elements in the teacher evaluation rubric?
- What is possible?

Protocol—Part 1: Reaching Consensus—7 Steps

Step 1   Schedule 60 to 90 minutes for whole staff to meet.

Step 2   Post the outcome so it is visible to entire staff:

Posted outcome: "Reach consensus on five things to look for in every classroom every day."

Step 3   Principal states expectations for outcome: "By the end of this hour, we will agree on five things—practices, behaviors, and actions—that must be in all our classrooms every day to support all students understanding of standards and overall learning."

Step 4   Principal asks, "If each of us and our parents were to walk into any classroom at our school, what should we see and hear? Based on your knowledge, experience, professionalism, and wisdom, what five things do you believe that students and teachers should be doing each day to support students' learning?"

- o *Individually*—Write one behavior, practice, or action on a sticky note.* Use as many sticky notes as you want. (2–3 minutes)
- o *Table Group*—Each person puts the sticky note(s) in the middle of the table and clusters sticky notes into themes (e.g., student engagement, teacher questioning). Table group agrees on five things, writes on chart or poster paper, then posts so all can see. (20 minutes)

Troubleshooting Tip: Ensure teachers write the five things with dark marker so they are visible to all in the room. Most groups want to put the sticky notes on the poster, which aren't visible to others.

Step 5 Identify five practices that should be in every classroom every day. Facilitators ask teachers to look at the state teacher evaluation document and study two domains that evaluate teacher effectiveness in the classroom. While teachers are studying, reading, and talking about the domains in their table groups, facilitators look at all the charts of the five practices posted by table groups and identify five practices that occur with the greatest frequency across all posters. Facilitators write the five practices on a new poster to offer to the group.

Step 6 Look at research. Use the state teacher evaluation document to determine if the five practices the group chose are substantiated by research. Because the state teacher evaluation document is based on research on effective teaching (Danielson, 2013), the group now matches their beliefs about teaching to research on effective teaching. This will determine if the five practices they chose will likely result in increased student learning.

Note: Other research options to consider for aligning the five practices from teacher beliefs to research may include: Research findings from *How People Learn* (National Research Council, 2000) and *Framework for Teaching* (Danielson, 2013).

Step 7 Revise the list of the five practices or keep it the same. Is our list of five supported by research? What should we change?

Facilitator Transition Statement from Part 1 to Part 2

How will each of us find time to learn to be highly effective at these five things?

Part 2—Selecting the Learning Design

The purpose of Part 2 is for teachers to select a "learning design" from a menu of nine designs. Each research-based design is implemented using a three-hour cycle that includes planning, enacting in the classroom, and assessing and revising (see Chapter 3 for detailed descriptions of the nine learning designs). Teachers choose the learning design based on interest and need for learning more about the five agreed-on practices—or the Five Agreements—that should be in every classroom every day. (See Chapter 4 for specific, concrete details on why teachers chose specific designs.)

Protocol—Part 2: Selecting the Learning Design—7 Steps

Step 1   Agree on purpose—why select a learning design?

Say: "We know that for each of us to be highly effective at the five practices we've chosen to be in every classroom everyday, we have to determine what changes in practice are needed, learn how to do those things using standards for professional learning, and practice together in the classroom to see changes in student results. What learning designs could we choose? How does each of us select a learning design that engages us as adults in the learning?"

Step 2   Offer names of learning designs and protocols for implementation. Write the name of a learning design at the top of a piece of poster paper with a picture of the cycle for implementing the learning design. A graphic representation was drawn on each poster showing the cycle of implementing the learning design— planning outside the classroom, teaching together inside the classroom, reflecting on results outside the classroom.

Nine learning designs were offered to each school in the study:

- Collaborative Planning, Teaching, and Assessing
- Peer Teaching
- Vertical Team Study

Figure 2.2   Learning Design Cycle

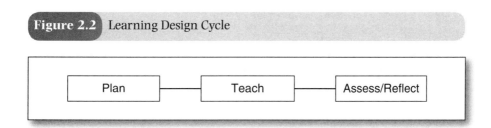

- Intentional Practicing with Student Response
- Using Technology—Linked-In Lessons
- Studying Video and Application
- Lesson Design
- Shared Learning with Teachers, Principals, and Coaches
- Creative and Innovative Teaching

Step 3 Describe what one cycle of the learning design looks like in practice.

- Planning—one hour
- Teaching—one hour
- Reflecting on results, assessing student understanding—one hour

Step 4 All teachers sign up for one of the learning designs. Teachers put their names on one of the learning designs posters.

Step 5 Schedule a time to implement one cycle in the fall and one cycle in the spring before the testing window. One principal brought monthly paper calendars (September–May) and asked teachers to sign up on for dates to implement Learning Design Cycles 1 and 2.

Step 6 Identify both text and human resources needed, such as participation by instructional coach, content knowledge expert, or principal.

Step 7 Schedule a date in May for the "Knowledge Showcase."

Part 3—Implementing the Learning Design Cycle

The purpose of Part 3 is for teachers to engage in two cycles of professional learning.

Each cycle has three parts and takes about three hours to complete.

First hour—Teachers or instructional coach meet for an hour to plan for the classroom experience. For example, the group that chose Peer Teaching is planning a lesson, while the Video Study group watches video, studies the practice they want to implement in the classroom, and plans a lesson that integrates the new learning into the lesson.

Second hour—Teachers implement the collaboratively designed lesson or new practice in the classroom.

Third hour—Teachers reflect on the outcomes and changes that occurred because of implementing the new learning in the classroom and assess student understanding.

Protocol—Part 3: Implementing the Learning Design—8 Steps

Step 1   Teacher teams meet on the designated date and time they agreed to in Part 2.

      o Cycle 1—implemented between September and November
      o Cycle 2—implemented between January and February before the teaching window

Step 2   Teachers meet outside the classroom for one hour and plan to implement new learning in the classroom. Use the district's/school's planning template.

Step 3   Teachers schedule a time to implement the lesson or practice the new learning in a teacher's classroom.

Step 4   Teachers meet in the classroom to implement the new practice. Each person's role is clear. One or two teachers facilitate the lesson, and one teacher records student responses to the new learning through writing or videotaping the lesson.

Step 5   Teachers meet for one hour outside the classroom and complete the reflection questions (see "Reflection Questions Cycle 1" template, remembering to document knowledge to remember which will be included in the PKB).

Step 6   Reflection questions are housed in one designated location for easy access and retrieval.

Step 7   Check-in—December or January, just before or after holiday break. Whole school staff meets and reflects on successes and challenges with implementing Cycle 1 of their chosen learning design.

      o What did they learn?
      o What would they change?
      o How will teachers continue to build on successes and address challenges?
      o What has changed because of what was learned in Cycle 1?

Step 8   Implement Cycle 2 (repeat Steps 2–6).

Part 4—Sharing Professional Knowledge With Whole School Staff

The purpose of Part 4 is for teachers and instructional coaches to share their newly acquired knowledge publicly. By collaborating during learning design Cycles 1 and 2, teachers create a social support system to examine their practice, have their practice examined by other teachers, and have an opportunity to share their new learning. The Knowledge Showcase will help to create whole school accountability and commitment for producing knowledge with professional learning that supports student learning.

Protocol—Part 4: Protocol Sharing Professional Knowledge—4 Steps

Step 1 Schedule a date at the end of the school year for the Knowledge Showcase.

Step 2 Each team meets to study the data and analyze findings.

- What did they learn?
- What changes were made in the classroom because of their new learning?
- What changes did students make?

Step 3 Each team prepares a way—PowerPoint, Prezi, poster, video—to share learning with whole school staff from engaging in Cycles 1 and 2 of their chosen learning design.

Each team has fifteen minutes to share.

Step 4 Whole school staff meets on the designated date(s) (see Step 1) and shares their learning from participating in Learning Design Cycles 1 and 2. Make visible the Five Agreements—those practices that teachers agreed to should be in every classroom every day—and reinforce the connection between teachers learning to the Five Agreements, which also align with teacher evaluation domains.

Part 5—Creating a Professional Knowledge Base

The purpose of Part 5 is to build a practitioner knowledge base that can be accessed and shared widely among the school staff and across the district. We learn from Hiebert, Gallimore, and Stigler (2002) that to improve teaching in a "steady lasting way, the teaching profession needs a knowledge base that grows and improves" (p. 3).

- How can teachers not lose what they have learned through implementing new practices in the classroom?
- How can practitioner knowledge be stored and shared for easy retrieval?

o How can new teachers benefit from the learning of other teachers that came before them?

o How can an incoming principal use the Knowledge Base to assess the culture of the school's learning climate?

Protocol—Part 5: Creating a Professional Knowledge Base–3 Steps

Step 1   Choose a person to coordinate the development of a database system for storing knowledge based on learning from Learning Design Cycles 1 and 2.*

Step 2   Choose a form for storing professional knowledge. This can be in a database system, which includes electronic files, lessons, and video that are indexed for easy access and retrieval. The idea is that there are strategies and examples of practice that teachers can see and use.

Step 3   Directions and expectations for using the school's knowledge base are written and clearly communicated to whole school staff and district administrators.

Troubleshooting Tip: Step 1 is essential for ensuring the PKB becomes a reality. Because Part 5 occurs in May or June at the end of a school year, when principals, teachers, and instructional coaches are exhausted, it is recommended that practitioner knowledge to remember be documented in the PKB throughout the school year, after the completion of each Learning Design Cycle. As one principal stated, "We have six days left. Our snowball is starting to roll really, really fast down the hill right now." She followed up with directions to the staff on report card entries into the new database system. It is, however, easy to forget when things get busy. There has to be a plan to create and archive the Knowledge Base throughout the school year and not wait until the end of the year, and a person to make sure it happens. Suggestion: Schedule a meeting with one teacher from each design team after each Learning Design Cycle, so everyone does not have to wait until the end of the year to formalize the Knowledge Base.

What is the timeline for implementing the FPP?

July–August

- Part 1—"Reaching Consensus" Protocol—60 minutes
- Part 2—"Selecting the Learning Design"—30 minutes

September–November

- Part 3A—Implement Cycle 1 of the Learning Design—180 minutes

January

- Check-in—20 minutes
- How is the plan going?
- What are you learning?
- What do we change—keep doing, stop doing, or start doing?

January–February

- Part 3B—Implement Cycle 2 of the Learning Design—180 minutes

May

- Part 4—Sharing Professional Knowledge Showcase with Whole School Staff. Choose a date in May for teachers to share learning from participating in the two learning cycles—120 minutes
- Part 5—Creating a Professional Knowledge Base

Select a person to schedule a meeting with one teacher from each learning design team for two purposes: (1) gather professional knowledge to archive and (2) select a place to archive the knowledge electronically allowing easy access to all teachers.

What does the FPP look like in practice?

Stories From the Field

Four schools—one high school math department and three elementary schools—implemented the FPP during one school year. Each school engaged in Parts 1 and 2 of the FPP before students arrived, agreed to five practices that should be in every classroom every day, and aligned the five practices with teacher evaluation domains (learning environment and teaching for learning). Each of the schools' teachers also chose learning designs to deepen understanding, knowledge, and skill to become proficient with each new practice (see Table 2.1).

All four schools had a principal or assistant principal to create the supportive conditions for implementing the plan, and a teacher leader/instructional coach "linchpin" at each campus who followed-up and maintained momentum. Each school enjoyed multilevel support for educator growth that encouraged continuous improvement during the design cycles of learning. Both the teacher leader and the principal roles proved essential

Table 2.1	Five Agreements and Learning Design Choices

School	Five Agreements	Learning Design Choices
Chavez High School	• Summarize every day • Use interactive notebooks • Use high-level questioning • Student work has meaningful feedback • Use word wall with visual representation	• Video Study with Application • Peer Teaching • Lesson Design • Collaborative Planning, Teaching, Assessing
Gainfield Elementary	• Students actively engaged • Students using of content vocabulary • Positive learning environment • Differentiated instructional for diverse student learners • Use learning targets daily	Video Study: K–2, 3–5
Hamos Elementary	• Teachers and students engaged in learning and assessment • Positive Learning environment • Students question, defend their thinking, and talk about content • Lesson goals and objectives are clear • Small groups/differentiated instruction	• Video Study with Application • Using Technology • Lesson Design/Vertical Team Study • Innovative and Creative Teaching • Vertical Alignment (2)
Terra Elementary	• High levels of student engagement • Language-rich environment, content vocabulary • Evidence of understanding using questioning and student modeling • Collaborative, cooperative learning environment where students are respectful and have ownership of their learning • Encourage problem solving and critical thinking skills	• Vertical Team Study • Video Study • Collaborative Planning, Teaching, Assessing • Using Technology

for implementation of the plan. Before school started, the principal knew the "nuts and bolts," that is, the mechanics of how the FPP could provide teachers with time and opportunity for professional learning and how this structure aligned to teacher evaluation. The teacher leader served as the linchpin that connected this vision to its realization—the person who initiated planning sessions, facilitated the design-cycle process, and invested energy in follow through actions vital to sustaining implementation. In other words, the teacher leader/instructional coach "kept it going." (See Chapter 9 for details about each school's story of enactment.)

SUCCESSES WITH IMPLEMENTATION

Chavez High School—Nine high school mathematics teachers actively engaged in Parts 1 through 5 of the plan. What teachers valued most was time for collaboration, especially planning and teaching together in each other's rooms. They also valued the Five Agreements as focal points for learning throughout the school year.

Gainfield Elementary—The entire school, about twenty teachers, engaged in Parts 1 through 3 of the FPP. What teachers valued most was the whole school focus, time for collaboration, and having time to study videos, practice, and apply in practice.

Hamos Elementary—Whole school staff, eighteen teachers and an instructional coach, participated fully in Parts 1 through 5 of the FPP. What teachers valued most was vertical collaboration. Each of the five learning design teams represented at least two grade levels. Examples: Early Childhood (EC)/Kindergarten to Grade 1, and Grade 1 to Grade 2. Hamos was the only school of the four where every learning design team had vertical representation, and was the only school where the Creative and Innovative Design was selected by two teachers.

Terra Elementary—The whole school, about thirty teachers, actively engaged in Parts 1 through 5 of the FPP. What teachers valued most was the whole school focus, time for collaboration, opportunity to choose designs, planning, learning from vertical connections with other teachers, and sharing with each other at the end of the year.

Despite the fact that the school's dynamic, highly effective principal was reassigned to a "turnaround school" for the upcoming year, the leadership team voted to implement Professional Learning Designs (PLD) (their term for the FPP) for the upcoming year. Their PLD plan will maintain a focus on teacher choice and collaboration, and the Five Agreements. One change will be made to the FPP—the focus will be on vertical integration and learning across the school. Teachers get to choose their PLD but have to actively engage in the design a cross grade level.

CHALLENGES WITH IMPLEMENTATION

Chavez High School—Time, multiple initiatives, and school demands on teachers' time was their greatest challenge. "Planning took longer than I thought. I kept thinking about the lesson!"

Gainfield Elementary—Demands and initiatives prevented the school from engaging in Parts 4 and 5 of the FPP. In March, the school was notified by district administrators that they would be part of a university "turn-around school program" resulting in extensive time and preparation for the upcoming year. The principal and instructional coach couldn't find the time for staff to meet for Parts 4 and 5 as they were in intensive, overwhelming planning and preparation sessions to become a turnaround school.

Hamos Elementary—The only challenge expressed by the Hamos staff was, "Can we do the FPP next year?" The principal is retiring, and the school is participating in a turnaround school program. Despite the fact that all teachers actively engaged and gained knowledge of practice in the Learning Design Cycles, and enjoyed the experience, it is questionable whether or not the teachers can implement the FPP next year due to impending changes in leadership and turnaround school initiatives.

Terra Elementary—Teachers found that they over-planned, and stated and wrote repeatedly, "We didn't have enough time."

WHAT IS YOUR SCHOOL'S CAPACITY FOR IMPLEMENTING THE FIVE-PART PLAN?

Are you ready to implement the FPP at your school?

1. Schedule a thirty-minute strategic planning meeting with principal, teacher leaders, instructional coach, and a person who has knowledge about the FPP.

2. Ask the following questions:

   o If we implement the plan, what big picture do you see for your school and teachers?
   o If the FPP is implemented, what outcomes do you hope to see?
   o What data will we use to assess changes in improved practice? Did the teacher learning result in changes and improvements in teacher and student learning?
   o What resources (money for substitutes or assistants to cover classes) and structures (professional learning communities, learning teams, after-school study groups) do we have for teachers to engage Part 3—two cycles of learning designs connected to the classroom?
   o Who will provide support and keep the implementation of the FPP moving forward?
   o How can we use continual feedback as a basis for improvement?
   o Will the plan be perceived by staff as a support and enhancement for their learning or as just something else to do?
   o How many initiatives are being implemented, and how could the FPP support teacher learning within the initiatives?
   o Is the FPP a good fit for our school? Will it result in improved teacher practices and more effective student learning?

3. If the team feels that the FPP aligns with school goals, and the school has the capacity to implement the plan, the next step is to schedule a three-hour meeting with staff before school begins to facilitate Parts 1 and 2 of the plan.

SUMMARY OF THE FIVE-PART PLAN

Part 1   Schedule a time before students arrive. Use the "Reaching Consensus" Protocol with the entire school staff—60 minutes before school starts (to agree on what math classrooms will look like)

Part 2   Teachers select learning designs—could be a PLC, Lesson Design, Vertical Team, Peer Teaching, and so on—that interests them to study together, (The big idea here is that teachers get to choose)—60 minutes

Part 3   Teacher teams implement at least two cycles of their learning design—once or twice in the fall, once or twice in the spring (before testing)—180 minutes per cycle

Part 4   Whole school staff holds a Knowledge Showcase session in May to share their learning and its impact on students—90–120 minutes Each team shares learning—10–15 minutes per team

Part 5   Learning is archived and stored in a school-based PKB where new learning, strategies, and instructional practices are easily retrievable.

YOUR TURN—START THE CONVERSATION

- How can your school implement the FPP?
- What might be the benefits and challenges of implementing the FPP at your school?
- What support does your school need to respond to changing conditions and sustain implementation?
- What changes would you make to the plan and why? What outcomes would you hope to see?

Cycles of Learning **3**
Designs Connected
to the Classroom

"Active engagement is vital to an effective learning design."

—Stephanie Hirsh and Shirley Hord (2012)

"You don't change performance without changing the instructional core. The relationship of the teacher and the student in the presence of content must be at the center of efforts to improve performance."

—Richard Elmore (2004)

"We went to the same trainings, but it wasn't until we got in each others' classroom that we realized that we were all implementing differently and getting different results from students."

—Alana, elementary teacher

In this chapter, the following questions are addressed:

- Why do teachers need learning designs connected to the classroom?
- What are nine learning designs that are connected to classrooms?
- How does the learning design look when enacted?
- What is a cycle for implementing a learning design?

- What do teachers, coaches, and principals learn by participating in a learning design?
- How can you structure time to implement the learning design on your campus?
- How can you use the learning design at your school?

At the end of this chapter you will be able to

- identify reasons teachers need to actively engage in learning designs connected to the classroom.
- name nine designs for professional learning connected to the classroom.
- identify the purpose and reasons for using a specific design.
- visualize the design in practice using a protocol and reading stories from teachers.
- identify a cycle of learning using a specific design.
- identify what teachers, coaches, and principals learn by using the design.

Learning Designs featured in this chapter:

- Collaborative Planning, Teaching, and Assessing
- Peer Teaching
- Vertical Team Study
- Intentional Practicing with Student Response
- Using Technology—Linked-In Lessons
- Studying Video and Application
- Lesson Design
- Shared Learning with Teachers, Principals, and Coaches
- Creative and Innovative Teaching

STORY 1—A NEW TEACHER'S "TRAINING" EXPERIENCE

Raquel is a first-grade teacher in her second year of teaching. When asked about her experiences with professional development, she states,

> We get pulled out for so many trainings—teacher evaluation, the new math and literacy standards, new math textbook, using technology, e-book training, and on and on. Last month, I spent five days out of my classroom. If I get one golden nugget for something I can take back and use, I am happy.

Do you meet in professional learning communities (PLCs)?

Yes—only to look at data. We are a turnaround school and teachers must use the entire forty-five minutes of PLC time once a week to analyze data. We really have no time to collaborate.

How do you know what to do differently once you analyze the data?

We don't have time to talk about what to do differently. Looking at the data takes the whole time. We are told that "we are professionals" and can find time to figure out what to do differently.

Where do you learn about strategies that support your students' improvement?

We have to read or learn on our own. There's just no time during the school day.

Raquel's story is similar to many stories of teachers whose PLC has been "taken over" with mandated data analysis. Period. The idea behind offering teachers a menu of learning designs is to provide a structure—time, place, and purpose—for teachers to *learn* what to change in their teaching to get different results in the data. What if Raquel and teachers on her team had time designated during the school year to collaborate so they can learn to improve what to do differently? Would this possibly decrease stress, uncertainty, and anxiety in an already overwhelmed context of high-stakes accountability? And what would happen if teachers could select their learning design?

Examples of school systems continuing to operate with a few administrators at the district level choosing professional learning experiences *for* teachers instead of *with* teachers are highlighted throughout this book. When professional learning is seen as relevant by teachers under intense pressure to produce results in the current context of accountability, there is willing, active engagement by teachers. To the contrary, when professional learning is not seen as relevant by teachers under intense pressure to produce results in the current context of accountability, mandated attendance can lead to poor attitudes and disengagement by teachers. A strong case can be made that results in the classroom could be better if stronger alignment existed between teacher and student needs with professional learning experiences to meet the need. Allowing teachers' choice over their own learning promotes greater engagement, better attitudes, and, most importantly, better outcomes in the classroom. Professional learning for principals, instructional coaches, and teachers is most effective when the content and activities are relevant, meaningful, and authentic to their practice. Teachers especially enjoy collaborative learning in classrooms with other teachers.

After engaging in learning designs of their choosing, teachers offered the following comments:

> "This was one of the best experiences I ever had. I could see the activities in action in the classroom. I learned how students can question each other. I can take the activities back to my classroom to support students right away."

> "I understand that how students think about solving problems is different than how I thought about it. I learned how to ask questions to 'uncover' student thinking."

> "For the first time, I was able to stand back and listen to my students' different ways of thinking about the standards while someone else taught the lesson. I learned what their [students'] misconceptions were."

> "It is wonderful to co-teach with another teacher. I get ideas from him (her), and we learned how to engage students at a higher cognitive demand."

> "It was great to have time to apply a practice from the video 'My Favorite No.' My students are more engaged."

> "For the first time in my teaching career, I've been able to choose and create a learning place that is nearer to my passions for connecting children to others around the world."

Why do teachers need learning designs connected to the classrooms?

Teachers need learning designs that are physically connected to the classroom to ensure their learning is authentic, relevant, and meaningful for supporting students through teachers' change in practice, knowledge, and skills. It seems so obvious that teachers' primary learning place for gaining knowledge of student learning and practicing new skills would be in the "instructional core" (Ministry of Education, 2010)— where all the action takes place. Where do students spend many hours learning in school? In the classroom. Where do teachers implement new practices? In the classroom. Why shouldn't the classroom be the site for teacher professional learning? Two analogies come to mind about doctors and guitar players. Teachers' learning exclusively outside the classroom is like doctors learning to treat patients without access to patients.

Another analogy might be a guitar player studying video of people playing guitar or reading about playing the guitar, without ever touching a guitar. Since teachers spend over thirty hours per week in classrooms with students, shouldn't most of teacher learning be *inside* the classroom with students? The FPP intentionally includes time for learning designs to be connected to the classroom as part of a cycle of implementation: one hour learning outside the classroom (using data, studying, reading, planning); one hour inside the classroom (enacting the lesson, gathering student artifacts); and one hour outside the classroom (analyzing student data, giving and receiving feedback, reflecting, revising).

According to the Learning Forward *Standards for Professional Learning*, a "learning design integrates theories, research and models of human learning" that promote change in teacher effectiveness (Learning Forward, 2012, p. 40). Learning designs that are job-embedded with peers support transfer of the learning to practice. The three stories that follow do *not* use this approach but are all-too common.

STORY 2—THE DYNAMIC SPEAKER

A director of professional development at a regional educational center heard a "dynamic speaker" at a national conference. Without assessing the needs of educators or consulting others, the director contracted the speaker and scheduled two days of professional development for all regional district leadership teams. Visualize this scene: 250 educators, sitting with school leadership teams at round tables pushed together so that there is little space to walk through the chairs, using a two-inch, three-ring binder to locate handouts, listening to a speaker who spoke into a a microphone and used advanced technology. For two days, there was minimal table conversation and active engagement, accompanied by maximum listening to a speaker who was presumably well compensated for speaking to the masses showcasing his latest technological creations. The computer displays he commanded were impressive, but the "stand and deliver" teaching design he used was archaic. To be fair, a few evaluations indicated participants "enjoyed the show." What new knowledge and skills did educators learn?

What will change for students as a result of leadership teams spending two days in this "training"? What will improve?

STORY 3—NO FOLLOW-UP

An assistant superintendent contracted with an expensive professional development provider to "train" all elementary teachers in how to use the new reading program. Teachers were mandated to attend a two-day summer session without intentional follow-up sessions to support teachers with implementation at their school. As a result of everyone investing time, money, and effort, what is likely to change with no support?

STORY 4—ALL DATA, ALL THE TIME

In a large district, money for professional development was reduced significantly, resulting in only one design available for teacher learning—job-embedded collaborative meetings—such as PLCs now designated exclusively for data analysis, leaving teachers no time or structure for learning new strategies. If the only time teachers have to learn has been designated for "data analysis only," now what will change?

What is a teacher to do to grow professionally—to become a highly effective teacher inside the classroom—if the only available time to learn new things is outside the classroom, and that time is misaligned with intended goals?

Essential questions must be answered when making decisions about how, where, when, and what teachers learn and apply in the classroom to improve student results. How does the training engage the learners? How are metacognition, reflection, and modeling used? When teachers leave the session, what new knowledge, skills, and dispositions do they have, and what support do they now have for application into practice? Unfortunately, there are still school systems today where decisions about learning designs are made *for* teachers by district-level administrators to address teaching deficiencies, without teacher voice, and often require teachers to attend sessions outside their classroom. It is difficult to overstate the missed opportunity when we exclude teachers from the selection process.

Research and knowledge from experts in the field guided the choice for nine learning designs connected to teachers' classroom (Easton, 2008; Learning Forward, 2012). This menu of learning designs empowers teachers to have a sense of self-efficacy and human agency. This means that by choosing from these designs for professional development, teachers have influence on how they learned to carry out activities designed to attain specific educational goals, such as becoming "effective" as measured by the standards of teacher evaluation (Bandura, 2006a). All nine learning designs combine the research of Richard Elmore, who argues for the effectiveness of "learning in the instructional core" (Ontario Ministry of Education, 2010), and Mihaly Csikszentmihalyi, who sheds light on what optimal learning experiences look like (see Chapter 7). This research shows that the road to achieving desired changes in the classroom begins when teachers, coaches, and principals articulate a need for instructional change, then develop shared knowledge with designs situated in the classroom. Nine "learning in the classroom" designs were written to create a sense of "flow" for the professional educator who can then develop competence in a safe environment.

Flow is the term used to describe a learning experience that has meaning and is enjoyable to the participant even while her capabilities are being stretched to the limit (Csikszentmihalyi, 1990). For this optimal state of learning, or flow, to occur, there must be four elements: (1) clear goals, (2) required skills to reach the goals, (3) feedback on progress towards the goal, and (4) the ability to control the activity. Learning encounters that achieve this state enhance the quality of life. When, however, the learning design is too challenging or seen as too removed from practice, which in a teacher's case is the classroom, people move out of flow. Too little connection to practice, and educators are not motivated to participate. In short, the learning designs that are most likely to create positive outcomes are those that include educators' voices, promote knowledge acquisition for increased effectiveness, are relevant and meaningful, are job-embedded, and promote flow. Can teachers' choice in professional learning designs connected to the classroom lead to shared responsibility for results and positive changes in the classroom?

What are nine learning designs connected to classrooms?

Nine learning designs were offered to teachers during Part 2 of the FPP. Each design was research based, was designed for learning in the "instructional core" (the teachers' school and classroom), and included time for active engagement, reflection, application, feedback, and ongoing support.

Design 1—Collaborative Planning, Teaching, and Assessing

Lynda, an elementary school instructional coach at Mountain Oaks Elementary School (not one of the FPP schools) noticed from both state and short cycle assessment data that fourth-grade students' lowest mathematics scores were in the state standards' domain of number and operations with fractions. Lynda observed that teachers' use of instructional strategies were inconsistent with research on how students extend understanding with fraction equivalence, thereby limiting students' accessibility to mathematics designated in the state standards. Instruction involved too much time with "teacher telling" and not enough "questioning"—one the of Five Agreements whole school staff identified early in the year that should be in every classroom every day to support student learning. Teachers also asked what to use to plan lessons and guide instruction. Do we use the state standards, short-cycle assessment data (which were used in teachers' evaluation), or the new curriculum textbook? To what do we pay the most attention? It was clear that teachers needed time and experiences to clarify and guide instructional decision making and to learn how to use questions during the lesson. Lynda asked the fourth-grade team to participate in the Collaborative Planning, Teaching, and Assessing (CPTA) learning design to better understand how students extend understanding of fraction equivalence, align a lesson to state standards using effective instructional practices, apply practices in a lesson, and assess results. During CPTA, teachers do not critique each other's teaching. Instead, teachers and coaches together reflect and provide feedback on how to connect and apply new practices to promote student engagement. Enacting one cycle of CPTA takes approximately three hours. One hour is spent to co-design the lesson, one hour to teach the lesson in the classroom, and one hour to assess student comprehension of the content using the new practices.

Purposes of CPTA

- Align a lesson from any textbook or resource to the Common Core State Standards or state-specific standards.
- Deepen teacher content knowledge.
- Learn effective instructional practices.
- Apply a new practice related to the Five Agreements during a lesson.
- Identify how students will engage in the content of the lesson.
- Identify differentiation strategies to support diverse student access to content during the lesson.
- Draw on a shared educator knowledge base to improve practice.
- Assess students' understanding and misunderstanding of specific standards.
- Enjoy planning, teaching, and learning with colleagues.

Visualizing CPTA—The Protocol

Before actions for coach or teacher leader:

1. Identify teacher teams who signed up for the CPTA learning design.

2. Create a schedule for the teachers to implement the collaborative teaching design.

   o Plan—60 minutes
   o Teach—60 minutes
   o Assess—60 minutes

3. Substitute teachers may need to be scheduled or have a plan for an authorized person to supervise classes while teachers participate in the design.

4. Look at data (benchmark, state assessment, etc.). What data show this lesson is needed for professional learning?

5. Choose the lesson from the textbook, supplementary resource, or teacher design that will be collaboratively planned.

6. Make a copy of the lesson for each educator in the planning session.

7. Identify the teacher who will facilitate the collaboratively planned lesson.

Part 1—Planning Outside the Classroom—60 minutes

1. Look at the objectives of the lesson.

2. Check the state standards. How are the objectives of the lesson aligned with the state standards?

3. Study the standard. What do we need to know about the standard? What should students know and be able to do?

4. Identify the learning targets for the lesson. At the end of the lesson, the "student will be able to . . ."

5. Design a one-hour lesson using your lesson-planning template. What teacher and student action will occur during the first ten minutes of the lesson? Middle thirty minutes? Summary of learning—fifteen minutes? What strategies will be used to engage students and allow them access to the state standards?

6. Look at the Five Agreements aligned to the teacher evaluation instrument that the staff created during Part 1 of the FPP (see Chapter 2). Identify the focus of learning for the current lesson. Example: questioning techniques to deepen student understanding.

7. Identify 1 to 3 research-based strategies to enact during the lesson that support intended professional learning with student results.

Note: Teachers should choose 1 to 3 strategies that support the intended focus. Example: If "questioning to deepen student understanding" is the focus for learning, then what does research say are the techniques that get results? This is a time to intentionally include research-based questioning strategies.

Examples teachers used during implementation:

- Three research findings and implications for teaching from "How People Learn"
- Questions to deepen Common Core Standards for mathematics practices
- Strategies for increasing the level of cognitive demand
- Formative assessment strategies—exit tickets
- Use second language learner strategies—learning targets and criteria for success

Example: Teachers choose to use learning targets and criteria for success, questioning, and sentence frames to use during the lesson.

1. Identify evidence of student understanding to bring to the "Assessment" session after the lesson. Evidence includes student work samples, anecdotes, pictures of student work on iPad or phone, and exit tickets.

2. Decide how each adult will participate during the lesson. Do the teachers want to observe quietly? Do teachers want to interact with the students to ask them questions?

Note: During sessions, we agreed that "helping" students by "telling them how" was not acceptable. Asking questions to clarify or push student thinking was appropriate.

Part 2—Teaching Inside the Classroom—60 minutes

1. One teacher facilitates the collaboratively planned lesson.

2. Teachers name the strategy aloud so all students can hear it as it is being used.

Example: Teacher begins the lesson with learning targets and criteria for success. Teacher says, "Look at the lesson's learning targets. Read the learning targets aloud together. Read the criteria for success together.

   Talk with a partner. What do you think you will learn in this lesson? What might you be able to do at the end of the lesson?"

1. Teachers record student reactions and engagement with the intended strategies.

2. Teachers stop three minutes before the bell or end of class to give students the exit ticket.

Examples: Teacher says, "Let's go back to the learning targets. What do you know about . . . ? What was easy or hard for you to do during the lesson? What did you enjoy about the lesson today?"

3. Teachers collect student work samples or exit cards to bring to the assessment session.

Part 3—Assessing Outside the Classroom—60 minutes

1. The teacher who taught the lesson starts and shares first impressions of using the intended strategies and overall observations from the lesson. What do you remember? What was easy/hard about using the strategy?

2. Look at student work samples or exit cards.

3. Identify themes from students' comments.

4. How supportive were the strategies for students?

5. Identify next steps for students.

6. Reflect on "collaborative teaching." Was it a meaningful professional learning experience for you? What did you learn about _____? (This should be related to the Five Agreements and other intended strategies.) Would you willingly engage in the CPTA again or recommend it to other teachers as a design for professional learning?

Note: This is not a place to critique each other's teaching. Collaborative teaching is a place to learn and try new things together, focus on what students know and can do, and identify intervention strategies and support for continued student growth.

Story of Enactment

The fourth-grade team at Mountain Oaks Elementary describes the CPTA as a powerful place of learning for them. Teacher insights included (1) how to connect the short-cycle assessment data, curriculum resource, and state standards; (2) how learning targets and criteria for success can focus the lesson flow to maximize student access to the standards; (3) how asking specific questions can scaffold instruction; and (4) how different models for fractions can extend students' understanding of equivalencies. What do teachers say about their experiences with CPTA?

"I've learned more in this three hours that will be useful to my teaching than in all the professional development the district has had me go to this year."

"It's great to have time to learn with other teachers in the classroom."

"It's good to have another set of eyes and ears to observe the students."

Your Turn

- Practice designing your own CPTA learning experience with a grade level at your campus.
- Use the CPTA lesson design template to guide your design.
- Remember to ask educators to reflect on specific learning from the CPTA experience. What did I (we) learn? Could I (we) recommend CPTA for other educators? What can be added to my (our) educator Professional Knowledge Base (PKB)?

Design 2—Peer Teaching

Melinda and Marcos, two high school mathematics teachers, chose Peer Teaching as a long-awaited opportunity to learn with each other. Due to the tightly scheduled fast-paced structure of the school day, opportunities to teach together are not available to the two teachers. Failure rates in Algebra I classrooms are high, and they want to learn more about how high-level questioning—one of the Five Agreements—can be used to engage students during math lessons.

Purposes of Peer Teaching
(Same as CPTA but only two teachers are involved)

Visualizing Peer Teaching—The Protocol
(Same steps as CPTA)

Part 1—Planning Outside the Classroom—60 minutes
(Same steps as CPTA)

Note: The only difference between the Peer Teaching protocol and CPTA is that only two teachers are involved.

Part 2—Teaching Inside the Classroom—60 minutes
(Same as CPTA)

Part 3—Assessing Outside the Classroom—60 minutes
   (Same as CPTA)

Enactment

   As a result of engaging in the Peer Teaching learning design, the two teachers said, "What I find valuable is having another teacher in class to focus on what students are doing and how they respond to the questions. Some questions shut students down. Some open them up." "I was able to get teaching and questioning ideas from teaching with another teacher." Both teachers agreed that the Peer Teaching design was a meaningful learning experience, would not only participate in the design again, but would also recommend Peer Teaching for others.

Your Turn

   • Practice designing your own Peer Teaching learning experience with another teacher at your campus.
   • Use the Peer Teaching lesson design template to guide your design.

Design 3—Vertical Team Study

   Three kindergarten and three first-grade teachers needed communication between what they saw happening vertically in their classrooms during the second-year implementation of a dual language program at their school. Vertical pieces needing connection and ongoing communication between the K–1 teachers included strategies for shared expectations, student performance, consistency with implementation, and how to study and reflect on what students needed to be successful in the program. Students receive content instruction in one language one week, and content instruction in the other language the next week. For many students, this was the first time for learning content in one language, which might not be the students' first language. The teachers must collaborate to ensure students are learning the content language successfully.

   When the dual language program began the previous year, the principal set aside time for the K–1 grade teams to meet vertically; however, during second-year implementation, time to meet vertically was unavailable. When the K–1 grade teams learned that they could choose a Vertical Team Study professional learning design as part of the FPP, "they jumped on the chance to work together and talk about vertical pieces."

   The team chose to combine student engagement and vocabulary acquisition to increase math vocabulary during mathematically rich discussions, and to study specific discussion strategies to increase student engagement.

Purpose of Vertical Team Study

- Connecting content across the grade levels
- Creating coherence of implementation
- Communicating shared expectations for student achievement
- Supporting student's understanding across the grade levels

Visualizing Vertical Team Study—The Protocol

Part 1—Planning Outside the Classroom—60 minutes

- Identify the area of need for vertical learning.
- Identify the specific vertical learning focus.
- Set common goals using the Five Agreements to identify intentional learning.
- Identify resources, videos, research to study.
- Identify 1 to 3 research-based strategies to use during a lesson.
- Identify the "lesson flow" and where the strategies will be integrated in the lesson.
- Choose evidence of student understanding to being to the Assessment session.
- Decide how each teacher will participate during the lesson.

Part 2—Teaching Inside the Classroom—60 minutes

- One or more teachers facilitate the lesson.
- The teacher names the specific target or strategy used during the lesson so it is explicit to students.
- Observing teachers record student reactions and engagement with the intended strategy.
- Teachers collect student work samples and exit tickets to bring to the Assessment session.

Part 3—Assessing Outside the Classroom—60 minutes

- Share first impressions of using intended strategies and overall observations of the lesson.
- Look at student work samples, student observations, and anecdotes.
- Identify students' misconceptions and/or misunderstandings.
- Identify strategies to support student growth as measured by the state standards.
- Reflect on Vertical Team Study as a learning design. What did you learn that you can apply in your class?

Story of Enactment

The K–1 grade teams implemented discussion strategies during math lessons in each of the six kindergarten and first-grade classrooms. The principal secured a half-day substitute teacher for the six teachers twice during the school year to allow for maximum participation by the teachers. After engaging in the Vertical Team Study, the K–1 teachers state, "We recommend Vertical Team to others. Vertical Team allows for focused conversations, develops a shared goal with the team, and we are able to see practices that we learned put into practice with other teachers."

One teacher remarked, "I like having my own video, having reflection time with teachers, and I like being accountable with and to my peers—this [Vertical Team] is a structure to remind each other we can try something new. We were all scared—it's scary to have another team to observe you. I like the fact that we tried something new."

Your Turn

- Practice designing your own Vertical Team Study learning experience teachers at your campus.
- Use the Vertical Team Study template to guide your design.

Design 4—Intentional Practicing with Student Response

The whole school staff—124 educators—at Cornerstone High School (not one of the FPP schools) spent two days in the summer in a professional learning session designed to create awareness and build knowledge about how to use adolescent reading strategies in content instruction. At the end of the institute, teachers met in teams to answer the following question, "What strategies will you practice in your classroom?" Teams identified and documented 1 to 3 strategies to use during instruction in their classroom, and informed the principal and staff of those actions. The principal and staff developed a shared language and understanding of the names of the strategies and how the strategies look in practice. Facilitated by the school principal, content teams created a plan for intentionally practicing the new strategies in a supportive climate of trust and risk taking using reflection on action and feedback from students.

Purpose of Intentional Practice with Student Response

- Practicing a new strategy or skill
- Engaging students in the use of the new strategy or skill
- Eliciting students' response to the strategy or skill

Visualizing Intentional Practice with Student Response—The Protocol

Part 1—Planning Outside the Classroom—60 minutes

   1. Use data to determine need.

   Example: Cornerstone High School's data indicated student literacy scores were well below the state average.

   2. Study effective strategies or skills.

   Example: Cornerstone High School engaged in whole faculty study to increase adolescent literacy. Faculty attended a two-day institute where all teachers learned about content literacy based instruction and how to use strategies that support students.

   3. Decide which strategies to practice.

   Example: Teachers agreed to try three strategies (anticipation guide, partner reading, and exit slips) throughout the year during the first year of implementation. Even the athletic coaches and elective teams practiced the strategies!

   4. Practice using the strategies.

   Example: Choose the place in the lesson where the strategy is to be used. Name the strategy as it is being used so students can hear the name and identify it.

   5. Decide how to elicit student response to the strategy.

   Example: Choose a method to collect student response.

Part 2—Teaching Inside the Classroom—60 minutes

   1. Strategy or skill is explicitly named in the lesson.

   Example: Teacher says, "Today, you will use anticipation guides to assess what you already know about our upcoming unit of study."

   2. Students understand why the strategy is useful, how it is used, and when it is appropriate.

   Example: Teacher says, "Anticipation guides reveal what you already know and need to know about what you are about to study."

3. Teacher stops three minutes before end of class to give students a response card.

- Name of Strategy—how strategy helped/did not help you and why

Example: Anticipation Guides—did it help/not help you under-stand the learning today. How did it help or not?

Part 3—Assessing Outside the Classroom—60 minutes

1. Look at student response cards.

2. Categorize cards into Yes/No piles.

    Yes—strategy helped. No—strategy did not help

3. Categorize student responses into themes from the Yes pile.

4. Reflect on responses with at least one other person (coach, teacher, or principal).

5. What is the next step?

Story of Enactment

What do teachers say about learning using Intentional Practice with Student Response?

The majority of the teachers responded favorable to intentionally practicing the same 1 to 3 strategies. Comments included the following:

"I know what to do now."

"Getting students to respond to the strategy made them a part of the learning."

" Using the strategies really pulled our staff together. We had one thing that we all shared and could talk about. We finally followed through with something."

After two years of implementing adolescent reading strategies, liter-acy scores increased.

On my last day at Cornerstone High School after a four-year partner-ship, I was walking and engaging in a conversation with a senior student. I asked him, "What was the most powerful thing he learned in high school that he would use in college?" He said that ever since he was a freshman, he had learned "reading" strategies that helped him in all classes—even math. "They really work and I will use those strategies at the university. It was great that all my teachers used them."

Your Turn

- Design your own Intentional Practice with Student Response experience.
- Use the Intentional Practice with Student Response lesson design template to guide your design.
- Remember to reflect on the experience. What did I (we) learn? Would I recommend the strategy for other educators? What can I (we) add to my (our) PKB?

Design 5—Using Technology—Linked-In Lessons

Adrian and Alexa, second-grade teachers and San Andreas Elementary School (not one of the FPP schools), designed a lesson to share together. Adrian participated on the large urban district's second-grade team to create a scope and sequence for implementing state math standards. He had also helped to align math lessons to standards. Alexa wanted to visit his math classroom, but school policy mandated that teachers could no longer be pulled out of classrooms. Fortunately, Adrian discovered a way that technology could be used to "link-in" both classes so that Adrian could teach a math lesson on place value to both his and Alexa's classrooms at the same time. Adrian and Alexa used the "Linked-In" protocol to co-design a lesson, and share the lesson together even while each stayed with their own class. After the lesson, they used the same system to reflect on student on what learning occurred.

Purposes of "Linked-In" Lessons

- Identify changes in classroom instruction required to engage students.
- Share the enactment of a collaboratively designed lesson by connecting two or more classrooms using this technology.
- Use research-based strategies to support student understanding of standards.
- Identify instructional strategies that increase student engagement in the lesson.
- Practice a specific move related to curriculum, instruction, or assessment.
- Engage with colleagues about commonly enacted classroom lesson.

Visualizing Linked-In—The Protocol

Part 1—Planning Outside the Classroom—60 minutes

1.   Use data to determine the common lesson.

Example: Data shows that second-grade students struggle with place value understanding. What are the specific student struggles?

2.   Study

Example: What do we need to know about place value?

3.   Schedule 15 to 20 minutes for teachers to plan the lesson.

4.   Choose the lesson.
    o What is a lesson that would reveal students' understanding and misconceptions?
    o What is a lesson that teachers could best learn from by experiencing the same lesson together?

5.   Plan the lesson using state standards.
    o Use the planning template.
    o Identify specific research based strategies to enact during the lesson that support student engagement and understanding.
    o Example: Teachers choose to use place value models, learning targets and criteria for success, questioning, and sentence frames during the lesson.

6.   Choose a form of evidence to collect.

Example: What student work will we collect to assess impact?

7.   Choose the teacher to enact the lesson.

8.   Identify what the teacher who is not teaching is doing in the classroom.

Example: The teacher who is not teaching focuses the students' attention on the screen that shows the teacher in the other room teaching. The teacher listens and records how students engage with the task and documents misconceptions and understandings.

9. Schedule the date and time to teach the lesson.

10. Coordinate and prepare the technology to link one classroom to the other(s).

Part 2—Teaching Inside the Classroom—60 minutes

1. One teacher enacts the collaboratively designed lesson to his/her class and at least one other class via technology.

2. The non-teaching teachers are doing the following in their respective classrooms:

   o Focusing students attention on the screen
   o Walking around observing students engage with the task
   o Listening to and documenting student thinking
   o Paying close attention to the specific strategies teachers agreed to try
   o Records how students react and engage with the strategies

3. Teachers stop 1 to 3 minutes before end of class to give students an evaluation card. Today, your teacher tried 1 to 3 strategies so you could learn:

   o Name of Strategy—Like/Not like—strategy helped me learn to

Part 3—Assessing Outside the Classroom—60 minutes

1. Each teacher shares first impressions of the Linked-In lesson.

2. Look at student evaluation cards. What did students say?

3. What was the outcome of using the identified strategies?

4. How did the pre-planned strategies support student engagement and understanding of the standards?

5. Identify what to keep, start, and stop. What do we add to our PKB?

6. Identify next steps for students.

7. Reflect on Linked-In lesson. Was it an enjoyable professional learning experience for you? What did you learn? Would you do it again or recommend it to other teachers?

Story of Enactment

Adrian and Alexa learned that linking their classes together through technology enabled them to better understand their students' misconceptions and misunderstandings about place value.

They were able to share the same lesson and observe students in both classes, resulting in differentiation strategies that would support a range of learners.

According to Adrian and Alexa, "It [Linked-In Technology] was a valuable learning experience for both of us to share the same lesson." They added, "We learned that our students struggle with the same concepts. We're going to try to use more models of place value to deepen students' understanding."

Your Turn

- Design your own Linked-In experience.
- Use the Linked-In lesson design template to guide your design.
- Remember to reflect on the experience. What did I (we) learn? Would I (we) recommend Linked-In for other educators? What can I (we) add to my (our) PKB?

Design 6—Studying Video with Application (SVA)

Grace and Enrique are mathematics teachers at Chavez High School who watched a video titled "My Favorite No" from the Teaching Channel during a professional learning session. The video shows an eighth-grade teacher asking students to solve a problem. She then records their solutions on index cards, and learns from their mistakes. Grace and Enrique expressed interest in using this strategy in their classrooms, but could not find the time during their busy school schedule to implement this plan. During Part 2 of the FPP, however, teachers chose a learning design that best aligns with their learning needs. Grace and Enrique chose the SVA peer-teaching format so they could allot time to study the "My Favorite No" video and collaboratively plan and implement the strategy in their classrooms. The two teachers wanted to know how the strategy could be used to understand student thinking about a problem, and how this understanding could inform appropriate interventions where necessary.

Purpose of SVA

- Learning new strategies and skills from videos, such as the Teaching Channel
- Practicing a new strategy or skill with students in the classroom
- Engaging students in the use of the new strategy or skill
- Eliciting students' response to the strategy or skill
- Reflecting on student engagement with the strategy

Visualizing SVA—The Protocol

Part 1—Planning Outside the Classroom—60 minutes

- Choose a video to study based on intended learning aligned to data and to the Five Agreements (see Part 1—Five Part Plan).
- Study the video and identify specific strategy to implement.
- Plan a lesson incorporating the strategy.
- Plan a time to implement the strategy.
- Choose the teacher(s) to facilitate or co-facilitate.
- Decide what evidence of impact on students will be collected, photographed, or documented, and used in the Assessment session after the lesson.

Part 2—Teaching Inside the Classroom—60 minutes

- Implement the agreed-on strategy.
- Collect evidence of impact of the strategy on students.

Part 3—Assessing Outside the Classroom—60 minutes

- Share evidence of impact on students by implementing the strategy.
- Share what you learned and what you found valuable about your professional learning experience in the SVA learning design. Would you engage in this learning design again? Would you recommend the learning design for other teachers? Why or why not?

Story of Enactment

Grace and Enrique implemented "My Favorite No" in Enrique's geometry class with the bell ringer problem: The diagonal of a square is 20 cm. What are the side lengths of the square? The teachers collaborated on choosing the student's solution to be the "favorite no." Grace showed the "favorite no" on the doc camera, then students engaged in table group conversations to identify what was correct in the solution and also identify the mistake. In ten minutes, students correctly identified the mistake and learned five different approaches to identifying side lengths of a square knowing that the diagonal is 20 cm. What did Grace and Enrique find valuable by engaging in the SVA learning design? "We enjoyed planning and teaching together." "We learned what students know and don't know in a short amount of time—what could be improved and how to reteach on the spot."

Your Turn

- Plan a cycle of SVA using the planning template.
- Which videos have been used with teachers at your school site?
- Where can videos that can be used as teaching tools be accessed easily by teachers?

Example: Teaching Channel

Design 7—Lesson Design

One first-grade and five second-grade teachers, while implementing a new mathematics resource, wanted to understand how to align lessons in the new resource with the Common Core Standards for Mathematics. Interpretations differed among the teachers about how lessons in the textbook aligned to the standards, and about the meaning of specific math vocabulary terms. Sondra, a second-grade teacher, states, "When we first started, several of us said that we hate this program—it just jumps from one thing to another. This textbook is not geared toward the Common Core, even though it says it is." Two of the teachers had participated previously in a formal Japanese Lesson Design, and believed that by designing in a lesson guided by a research question and followed by data collection, the teachers would gain an understanding of how to align lessons from the new textbook to the Common Core Standards, and then share this knowledge vertically.

Purpose of Lesson Design

- Working collaboratively to strengthen a group designed lesson
- Designing a research question
- Teaching the lesson to get data on how well the lesson engages students
- Improving learning for all students

Visualizing Lesson Design—The Protocol

Part 1—Planning outside the classroom—60 minutes

- Identify a teaching problem based on student needs and establish an overarching goal.
- Develop a research question.
- Design a lesson
- Focus the lesson on student thinking, learning, and misunderstanding.

- Build a context for the lesson.
- Identify learning targets and criteria for success.
- Engage students with concepts.
- Design a way for students to share their thinking.
- Identify evidence to collect to assess student learning of the target.

Part 2—Teaching Inside the Classroom—60 minutes

- Enact and observe the lesson.
- One teacher facilitates the lesson, the other teachers observe and document student thinking. NOTE: Teachers do not interact with the students.
- Collect evidence of student thinking, such as work samples, pictures, videos, anecdotes, and student conversations.

Part 3—Assessing Outside the Classroom—60 minute

- Debrief, reflect, and revise the lesson based on the data collected.
- Evaluate the lesson's impact on student learning.
- Share the results.

Story of Enactment

As a result of engaging in Lesson Design, teachers say,

We learned how to design a research lesson together, we now share the same academic language for different graphs and can distinguish the difference in the graphs, and have learned from our colleague how students engage in questioning each other.

Sondra stated, "We've learned how to use the resources more effectively so it connects with the standards. We are very excited that we got to engage in two cycles of Lesson Design."

Your Turn

- Plan a cycle of Lesson Design using the planning template.

Design 8—Shared Learning with Teachers, Principals, and Coaches

Michael and Sophia, fourth-grade teachers at Lamott Elementary (not one of the FPP schools), wanted to ask questions that invite student participation in discussions. During a professional learning session, they learned six questions that guide students' thinking and intended to try them in a lesson so they could collect feedback on how students responded. Individually,

Michael and Sophia struggled to get students to talk and frequently heard students respond with "I don't know" to their questions. Melissa, the principal, and Serena, the coach, observed that many teachers struggle with questions that invite student participation. Michael and Sophia's concern is how to respond with the "right" question that invites students to talk, and that they do not answer the question for students. Michael, Sophia, Melissa, and Serena chose to use the "Shared Learning" design to participate in a common experience to learn how students engage with the questions.

Purpose of Shared Learning with Teachers, Principals, and Coach

- Gaining understanding of a new practice
- Observing the new practice in action
- Developing a shared understanding of how the new practice looks when used with students
- Observing students' engagement with the new practice
- Identifying assistance needed for being successful with the new practice

Visualizing Shared Learning with Teachers, Coaches, and Principals— The Protocol

Part 1—Planning Outside the Classroom—60 minutes

1. Coach or teacher schedules a time to for teacher(s), coach, and principals to meet.

2. Coach or teacher informs principal of meeting date and place.

3. Teacher begins by describing the sequence of the lesson, and informs the coach and teacher about the 1 to 3 new practices to try during the lesson.

4. Questions and concerns are posed about the new practice.

5. Teacher clarifies roles during the lesson.

   Example: Holly and Sophia will co-teach the lesson. Melissa and Serena will listen for teacher questions and student responses, then document on a template.

Part 2—Teaching Inside the Classroom—60 minutes

1. The teacher(s) enacts the collaboratively designed lesson focusing on trying the new practices.

2. Coach and principal observe teachers using the new practice and how students respond and engage.

3. Coach and principal document evidence of the new practice in action.

4. Teachers stop three minutes before end of class to give students an evaluation card. Today your teacher tried a new strategy so you could learn:

Name of Strategy—Like/Not like—strategy helped me learn to . . .

Part 3—Assessing after the Lesson—60 minutes

1. Teachers, coach, and principal meet for twenty minutes.

2. Each person shares first impressions of the Shared Learning lesson.

3. Principal and coach share their observations and evidence about how the new practice looked in action.

4. Look at student evaluation cards. What did students say?

5. What was the outcome of using the identified strategies?

6. What assistance is needed to support using the new practice?

7. Reflect on Shared Classroom learning. Was it an enjoyable professional learning experience for you? What did you learn? Would you do it again or recommend it to other teachers? Why?

Story of Enactment

After engaging in a cycle of the Shared Learning design, teachers, principals, and coaches said . . .

Teacher—"My principal and coach were learning alongside me and not evaluating me. I'm a first year teacher and this felt really supportive."

Teacher—"It felt like there were really three teachers in the room. I didn't know my principal knew so much about instruction. It was very helpful."

Coach—"It felt good to share the learning with everyone (teachers and principals) and to see the kids so actively engaged. It had that community feel."

Principal—"It was a treat to step out of my 'evaluation' role to focus on instruction and enjoy learning with the teachers."

Your Turn

- Design your own Shared Learning opportunity.
- Use the Shared Learning planning template to guide your design.
- Remember to reflect on the experience. What did I (we) learn? Would I recommend Shared Learning for other educators? What can I (we) add to my (our) PKB?

Design 9—Creative and Innovative Teaching

Endia and Dea, a kindergarten teacher and Head Start Facilitator, intended to try out a multidisciplinary project that would connect the students in their rural farming community to students in other countries in a positive way. Their plan was to raise the money needed to purchase and ship "indestructible" soccer balls to students in parts of the world that had few resources. For quite some time, Dee had wanted to implement the yearlong project to engage students in community projects so they could learn to give to others through teamwork, develop appreciation and respect for diverse cultures, and learn to live a healthy lifestyle. She also wanted students to have a reason to develop writing and communication skills through an authentic experience. In this age of high-stakes accountability, there was no time or structure to try an innovation or ignite a passion. Dee asked, "How can we try a new project within accountability guidelines?" When teachers were given the opportunity to choose to enact two cycles of the learning design, they chose Creative and Innovative Teaching (CIT) to implement their idea.

Purpose

- Bringing fresh perspectives to teaching
- Trying new ideas in the classroom
- Recognizing diverse strengths and engage diverse students
- Expanding the possibilities for learning
- Problem solving new approaches when encountering difficulties
- Finding new ways to question, motivate, facilitate and guide all students to new heights
- Developing approaches that foster intrinsic motivation

Visualizing CIT—The Protocol

Part 1—Planning: 60 minutes

1. Identify the creative activity or innovation to try in the classroom.

2. Pose questions and concerns about the innovation.

3. Study research about the creative activity or innovation.

4. Design a lesson using the creative activity or innovation.

5. Clarify roles during the lesson.

Part 2—Inside the Classroom—60 minutes

1. The teacher enacts the innovative idea, activity, or process.

2. CIT members observe teachers using the innovation and how students respond and engage.

3. CIT members document evidence of the new practice in action.

4. Teachers stop three minutes before end of class to give students an evaluation card. Today your teacher tried a new strategy so you could learn:

   o Name of Strategy—Easy/Hard

Part 3—After the Lesson—20 minutes

1. CIT members meet for 20 minutes.

2. Each person shares first impressions of the innovation in action.

3. CIT members share their observations and evidence about how the new practice looked in action.

4. Look at student evaluation cards. What did students say?

5. What was the outcome of using the innovation?

6. What is the next step?

7. Reflect on CIT experience. Was it an enjoyable professional learning experience for you? What did you learn? Would you do it again or recommend it to other teachers? Why?

Story of Enactment

Endia and Dea's sharing at the Knowledge Showcase was powerful and inspirational! They used a PowerPoint presentation to share their story of enactment. Their presentation included goals for the "One World Football" project, activities to reach the goals, evidence of progress using videos and literacy data, and results. Endia and Dea planned 1 to 3 times weekly and infused activities in all academic areas aligned with Common Core Standards. The broad project goals were to develop respect, appreciation, and acceptance for one another. The more specific goals were to raise $40.00 to purchase two indestructible soccer balls for students: one for the class and one to be sent to children in a country who could not afford a soccer ball. Students raised money by exercising and performing kind acts for teammates. Progress toward the goal was graphed and students communicated progress with pen pals in another city. Writing skills aligned with the yearlong soccer ball project. Students met their goals: They earned the money for the two soccer balls, increased their literacy skills (90% proficient, up 20% from the year before), and "learned that even though they are small, they can help in big ways." Their learning connected with the Five Agreements, as Endia states, "by continually reviewing the project in academic areas, students had the opportunity to practice writing skills, verbalize what they learned showing understanding, and when children are interested, focused, and motivated—learning increases."

The FPP provided Endia and Dea the space to create and innovate. Without the structure of the plan, the One World Project would not have been possible.

Your Turn

- Design your own CIT experience.
- Use the CIT design template to design a session.
- Remember to reflect on the experience. What did I (we) learn? Would I (we) recommend CIT for other educators? What can I (we) add to our PKB?

What is a cycle for implementing a learning design?

Each learning design is implemented in a "cycle." This means that there is a predicable sequence of actions for each of the ten designs.

Step 1—Planning outside the classroom—1 hour

Step 2—Enacting in the classroom—1 hour

Step 3—Assessment/reflection—1 hour

Three structures were used to implement the three-hour cycle.

1. <u>Three-Hour Block</u>—Teachers and coach scheduled a three-hour uninterrupted time to engage in all three parts of the cycle—plan, teach, assess. Substitutes were required or classes were "covered" by another teacher. The principal would hire the substitute teacher

for the entire day (easier to get subs for a whole day rather than half a day) and ask one team to schedule one three-hour cycle in the morning and another team to schedule a cycle in the afternoon.

2. Planning/Assessing during Collaborative Time/Professional Learning Community—Teachers at one school engaged in Part 1 (planning) and Part 3 (assessing) of the learning cycle during collaborative team time or during their PLC, then scheduled a common time for Part 2 (teaching in the classroom) teachers at the other three schools to use their PLC time only for data analysis.

3. Planning after School—Teachers at three schools were required to use their PLC time for data analysis, so they found time after school to meet for engaging in Part 1 and Part 3 of the plan.

YOUR TURN—START THE CONVERSATION

1. What is the intended outcome for choosing a specific learning design?

2. How do teachers have choice in selecting the design?

3. What is the teacher's, coach's, and principal's roles in enacting the learning design?

4. What is the schedule for implementing the learning design?

5. Does the school have a climate of trust and collaboration for risk taking reflection? If no, what steps will move the school forward?

6. How will the success of the learning design be evaluated?

Table 3.1 Scheduling

August	• Introduce the design as part of school's overall professional learning plan • Teachers sign-up for one design • Teachers put time for implementing the cycle on the school's yearly calendar
October–November	• Teachers implement Cycle 1 of chosen learning design
January–February	• Teachers implement Cycle 2 of chosen learning design
May	• Teachers share findings with faculty at the Knowledge Showcase

7. How is teacher participation used as documentation of evidence on the state teacher evaluation system?

8. How is student learning changing because teachers participate in the learning design?

9. If the PLC or collaborative team time is used for data analysis exclusively, where, when, and how are teacher learning to do things differently to respond to the data?

The Power of Teachers Selecting Learning Designs 4

"Self-belief does not necessarily ensure success, but self-disbelief assuredly spawns failure."

—Albert Bandura

"Educators are responsible for taking an active role in selecting and constructing learning designs that facilitate their own and others' learning."

—Learning Forward (2012)

"When we implemented a Dual Language program, and our time to meet vertically was taken away, we jumped on the chance to select a learning design to talk about expectations, strategies, and student performance."

—Cathryn and Jerrilyn, K–1 teachers

In this chapter, the following questions are addressed:

- Why is there a need for teachers to select learning designs?
- How and why do teachers select learning designs?
- How can learning designs be connected to the teacher evaluation system?
- What happens when teachers have a voice in choosing learning designs?

At the end of this chapter, you will be able to

- name two reasons why teachers need to select job-embedded learning designs;
- identify why and how teachers select certain learning designs;
- identify how the Five-Part Plan (FPP) guides teachers in connecting learning designs to the teacher evaluation system;
- describe the impact on teachers when they have a voice in choosing learning designs; and
- know how to use a checklist in selecting learning designs.

WHY IS THERE A NEED FOR TEACHERS TO SELECT LEARNING DESIGNS?

<u>Reason 1</u>—Teachers need time and place to engage in job-embedded professional learning that supports continuous improvement as measured in the context of teacher evaluation.

<u>Reason 2</u>—Teachers need a greater sense of professionalism by strengthening teacher self-efficacy, agency, and ownership for their work.

Two experienced third-grade teachers at a "turnaround school," an intensive leadership intervention initiative that provides funds to help principals turn around failing schools (U.S. Department of Education, 2014) describe their eleventh and seventeenth years as "overwhelming." What follows is a snippet of their conversation:

- *Morale is so low. It seems like all we do is test. Last month, we tested students for eight days.*
  When you get the data, what do you do with it?
- *We meet in PLCs [professional learning communities] and analyze, analyze, analyze. We used to have time in PLCs to talk and learn new things. Now we just look at data.*
  How much time do you spend learning what to do to improve?
- *We have no time. When I try to shift the conversation to "what next," I get shut down.*
  Have you voiced this issue with your administrators?
- *We've tried but we're told that we must spend our entire PLC time analyzing data.*

When the two teachers and I engaged in this conversation, it was disturbing for several reasons. First, their story calls attention to the disparity in how much time students and teachers spend testing and how little time is allocated to finding ways to improve student results. It seems obvious that after teachers analyze data, they need time to explore *teaching quality*, to develop the type of instruction that enables all students to learn. Second, the teachers lacked self-efficacy in choosing the content of their job-embedded PLC. Proponents of self-efficacy, grounded in social constructivist theory, maintain that a critical ingredient to successful achievement of goals is that people be allowed to exercise some control over what they *do* toward achieving those goals. Teacher self-efficacy supports teacher beliefs in their own ability to plan, carry out activities, or influence outcomes toward educational goals (Bandura, 2006b). Because they were required to use all the PLC time for data analysis, no time was ever allotted to realize what should be the main purpose of a PLC—to strengthen teacher practice and increase student results. Third, when a teacher attempted to steer the conversation to discuss "what next," she felt "shut down" or denied the self-efficacy to generate any new ideas. Administrators disallowed meeting time to discuss interventions and different instructional strategies, and set a dismissive tone to chill future discussions.

The third-grade teachers' story illustrates an essential need for teachers in the current context of teacher evaluation—the need for time to learn to respond to data for different student results, and the ability to make decisions about their own professional learning. Research and common sense agree that students and teachers are better served when teachers have a regular time and place to engage in professional learning, and have some efficacy in what they learn. Clearly, a need exists to create a support structure for teachers to learn what to do differently *after* they analyze the data. No choice was offered to the teachers in selecting a time or place during their school day to respond to the data to attain better results. Even when schools do allocate one hour per week for teachers to meet in a PLC or learning team, in some schools, the teachers' PLC agenda is determined by upper-level administrators implementing mandates from above to support district initiatives.

Within the complex and ever-evolving context of teacher evaluation, where, when, and how are teachers learning to respond to data effectively? How do teachers learn what to do better to support students' growth and have a voice as professionals in decision making? There is an ever-growing need for job-embedded learning designs that respond to needs identified by teacher evaluation systems, and for teachers to grow professionally. To ignore this need for teacher growth is to risk stagnation.

Years of research show that effective teachers do matter for student performance. Two years with effective teachers can put students on a college track. Two years with ineffective teachers can cause a significant decrease in this achievement (Jordan, Mendro, & Weerasinghe, 1997).

State teacher evaluation systems are designed to promote teaching effectiveness to ensure that every child learns from effective teachers (Coggshall, et al., 2009; Danielson, 2013; Darling-Hammond, 2014). For all teachers to become effective, teachers need time for full integration of high-quality, job-embedded professional learning to learn the knowledge, skills, and dispositions necessary for change and improvement. Following the learning experiences must come support in the form of coaching, mentoring, or reflective partnership for applying new learning effectively in practice (Joyce & Showers, 2002).

Research on professional learning, PLCs, and effective teaching is compelling, substantive, and powerful (Hord, 2009; Darling-Hammond, 2014). We now know that when teachers have self-efficacy, learn as a team, and work collaboratively, student gains are most significant. When this kind of learning is in place, great leaps can take place in student achievement. If we heed this research, what exactly will that look like, and how can teachers like the two third-grade teachers mentioned earlier experience structured, meaningful learning? How can we create a system for teachers to learn connected to their classroom, experience self-efficacy in selecting learning designs, and promote continuous learning for them and, ultimately, for their students? The FPP is a systemic approach to answering these questions.

HOW AND WHY DO TEACHERS SELECT LEARNING DESIGNS?

From my thirty-plus years of educational experience in six states, I have learned that, despite the research, most school systems' administrators choose professional learning for teachers based on "teacher need" without ever asking for teacher input. Administrator decisions in teacher learning are often informed by perceived teacher deficiencies or to further a state or district initiative. Why might this be despite the aforementioned research that supports teacher self-efficacy? It seems that teachers are not trusted to make appropriate decisions to support their students' learning needs. Why have decision makers not considered using the teacher voice? I remember my years as a classroom teacher when I was often told where to go on my "PD days" and what time to be there, yet was never involved in the selection process. State and national conferences offered a refreshing exception to this rule. The large conferences were often delightful in large part because I could select sessions that interested me, or ones that I needed more skills to support my students. I want to acknowledge that trends in professional learning are changing positively, in large part due to the research and expertise of organizations like Learning Forward. They are shaping professional learning internationally to include teacher voice for active engagement and providing standards that guide decision making with effective results.

One key learning from implementing the FPP is that when teachers have the opportunity to select a learning design, the selection is purposeful, relevant to their professional and student needs, and meaningful for them in some way. As the research suggests, teachers appear to make good choices, though the program is still in its infancy, and the data are limited. How and why do teachers make these choices? Using three data sources—teacher reflections, teacher interviews, and site observations from forty-one out of sixty-one teachers in the study—I found seven reasons teachers selected learning designs:

1. Continue existing collaborations that were taken away

2. Learn something new

3. Engage in a project or content they are passionate about

4. Plan and co-teach with colleagues

5. Build capacity for other grade level teachers to learn what they learned

6. Deepen understanding of a specific topic, such as student engagement, formative assessment, or differentiation

7. Implement the state standards using newly adopted programs and resources

Part 1 of the FPP asked whole school staff to accomplish two tasks:

1. Reach consensus on Five Agreements—five practices that should be in every classroom, every day that supports student learning based on educator experience and professional knowledge

2. Align five practices to teacher evaluation rubric domain elements

By engaging in a process to correlate Five Agreements with the teacher evaluation rubric, school staff discovered that every one of the five practices they believed should be in every classroom everyday aligned in some way to elements in three domains:

Domain 1—Preparation and Planning
Domain 2—Creating an Environment for Learning
Domain 3—Teaching and Learning

Part 2 of the FPP invites teachers to select a learning design from a menu of nine designs, where they could deepen their understanding of knowledge and skills to become effective/highly effective on one or more of the Five Agreements. (See Chapter 2 for a more detailed description.)

In the first year of implementation of the FPP, how and why did teachers from four schools select specific learning designs?

1. *Opportunity to continue existing collaborations*—Jerrilyn, kindergarten teacher, and Cathryn, first-grade teacher, along with their grade-level teams, jumped on the chance to have time for continued vertical communication during their second year of implementation of a dual language program, therefore, the K–1 teams selected Vertical Team Study as the appropriate learning design. During the first year of implementation of the dual language program, time was allocated for the teams to meet and discuss the "vertical pieces that all English Language Learners would need to be successful in the program" specifically, "strategies, expectations, and student performance. We needed the team to collaborate to make sure students were learning the content language." Beginning the second year, no time was set aside for the teams to meet. When offered a menu of learning designs, the team intentionally chose the appropriate design—Vertical Team Study—to achieve their goals for effective implementation of the dual language program. Selecting the design gave the teachers 9 to 12 hours of time during the year to communicate, reflect and refine their practices, and assess and evaluate student performance. (See Chapter 3 for more information.)

2. *Time to learn something new*—Two vertical teams at Hamos Elementary want time to learn something new about technology. Team 1—preschool, kindergarten, and first-grade teachers—set a goal to become more skilled at supporting students vertically through the use of technology. As a result, actively engaging in two cycles of the technology learning design, students increased their use of Leap Pads (learning tablets for children), which are used to increase hand–eye coordination, fine motor skills, numeracy, and early reading and writing skills. Individual student profiles are set up, and progress is monitored. Team 1 holds family nights to explain the technology, and parents and students are provided tutorials to learn how to use Leap Pads and computers at home. Throughout the school year, teachers communicate with parents via text messages or e-mail in addition to traditional paper notes, to remind them of important events (family–teacher conferences, meetings, programs) and share information related to individual student progress. Team 2—instructional coach, kindergarten,

and first-grade teachers—sets the goal to learn how to use the SMART Board more effectively for different levels of student learning by increasing teachers' ability to design SMART Board activities, and for both student and teacher to have fun in the learning process. Learning in this technology design connected with the Five Agreements as follows: increase student and teacher engagement, increase questioning at higher levels by both teachers and students, and develop the ability to differentiate instruction through modeling.

3. *Engage in a project they are passionate about*—One of the kindergarten teachers and soccer coach is passionate about fitness, students' written expression and communication skills, and connecting students globally. The teacher and the Head Start facilitator selected the Creative and Innovative Teaching design as an opportunity to enhance their creative energies by implementing a yearlong interdisciplinary project integrating literacy, social studies, mathematics, technology, and fitness. India wanted to know how a real-world experience focused on giving to others, developing respect and appreciation for one another, encouraging acceptance for diverse cultures, and learning to live a healthy lifestyle could be connected to Common Core Standards and accountability. When the teachers got the opportunity to select a learning design, they chose a project that actively engaged students, promoted physical fitness, and increased student achievement in literacy. (See Chapter 3 for additional results.)

4. *Plan and co-teach with colleagues*—Two teams of high school math teachers chose Peer Teaching as a way to learn with other colleagues by planning lessons, teaching together, and assessing/reflecting on the outcomes. The reasons teachers selected the Peer Teaching design included the following:

> What I find valuable is having another teacher in class to focus on what students are doing.

> Getting ideas from teaching with another teacher.

> We are excited to learn from each other. We said we wanted to be in each other's rooms but we don't get around to it. We plan great things and they get pushed back. Right now, we are intimidated to be in each other's classes. The "Peer Teaching" plan sounds less intimidating and we can provide effective feedback.

As a result of implementing the design, teachers value the opportunity to learn alongside colleagues and give and receive feedback.

5. *Build capacity for grade level teachers*—Two teacher leaders at Hamos and Terra experienced professional learning through the formal Lesson Design process, a professional learning process that Japanese teachers engage in systematically to examine their practice and become more effective. The teacher leaders sought to introduce Lesson Design to other teachers at their school, yet couldn't find a time prior to installing the FPP. Part 2 of the FPP—selecting a learning design—opened up the time and provided a structure for engaging in Lesson Design. Two teams selected Lesson Design for their learning design.

Team 1—Hamos: Five second-grade teachers and one first-grade teacher (two of the teachers teach in Spanish) chose a hybrid of Lesson Design and Vertical Team Study as "an experience and a way to improve student engagement and align their mathematics content vertically." One of the second-grade teachers stated,

> We implemented a new math program this year. When we started, we hated the program—it felt like we were jumping from one thing to another. How can we talk together to make this work and connect it to the Common Core Standards? We want to learn together—to have Lesson Design as part of our teaching and connected to the Five Agreements. We want vertical communication—there are things that first and second are doing that we all need to see.

(See Chapter 3 for additional details and results.)

Team 2—Terra: Three third-grade teachers saw an opportunity to better understand how students develop an understanding of the distributive property using research-based instructional strategies. With their design, they deepened their content knowledge of the distributive property through active engagement in the two cycles of Lesson Design. They also studied and applied two high-leverage practices—setting up and managing small group work and teaching a lesson or segment of instruction (Teaching Works, n.d.), and assessed student understanding by collaboratively examining student work samples.

6. *Support student learning*—Grace and her colleague, both high school mathematics teachers, saw the Teaching Channel video "My Favorite No" during a professional learning session focused on formative assessment, and wanted time to learn how to increase their understanding of two of the five agreements: (1) provide student work with meaningful feedback and (2) use of high level questioning. They selected a hybrid of two learning designs—Peer Teaching and Video Study with

Application—to meet their individual and team goals for learning "what students know and don't know and what can be improved." The teachers studied the video and planned a lesson to implement the strategy. Together they practiced the strategy, enacted the strategy in the class-room, and reflected and assessed results.

7. *Support for implementation of state standards*—The fifth-grade team at Terra Elementary selected Collaborative Planning Teaching and Assessing (CPTA) to find out why there was such a discrepancy in fifth-grade test scores in the geometry domain. They felt that after extensive data analysis, the CPTA would help them to collaboratively design the same lesson and uncover why some students were successful and some struggled. For Cycle 1, the team designed a lesson emphasizing ordered pairs and specific distances on coordinate planes. They discovered that each teacher had different methods and strategies for engaging students in the content. During Cycle 2, they identified which strategies supported student thinking more effectively than others, and implemented those with more consistent results.

Evidence from data sources indicates that teachers demonstrated positive affect and excitement about having the opportunity to select and actively engage in a learning design, not only in the beginning when they selected the design in August, but also at the end of the year after partici-pating in two "design cycles" for 6 to 12 hours. Teachers enjoyed collabo-rating and constructing learning about a topic meaningful and relevant to their needs, and learning deeply a topic about which they were passion-ate. Cathryn and Jerrilyn, two of six first-grade and kindergarten teachers who participated in Vertical Team Study, said,

> We recommend Vertical Team to others. Vertical Team allows for focused conversations, develops a shared goal with the team, and gives us an opportunity to learn and see practices aligned to teacher evaluation that we put into practice with other teachers.

Krista, the principal, stressed that

> teachers have choices as to what and how their learning takes place. I saw teachers selecting learning designs as a way connect professional development to teacher evaluation, put it in the class-room, and sustain that learning over time so we can see the effects in the classroom and with students—the place where you want to see the biggest impact of the PD.

Teachers choosing their own learning design, determining goals and outcomes, then organizing when and how the learning occurs (whose classroom, what dates) was consistently and overwhelmingly perceived by teachers as a refreshing and rejuvenating experience, described by Mihaly Csikszentmihalyi as "flow." Contrast teachers' positive disposition with their mostly inadequate "professional development" experiences described earlier in this chapter. Recall that district-level administrators or principals mandated these professional development activities for teachers. Teachers were engaged outside their classroom in content that may or may not be relevant for acquiring new skills to support student needs. Expensive, external consultants facilitated activities that did not integrate research, theories and models of adult learning, and were not followed up with support for implementation.

Summing up, the seven reasons teachers cited for selecting a specific design were grounded in advancing their professional knowledge through collaboration, and the act of "selecting" the design promoted teacher self-efficacy and autonomy—designs were chosen *by* the teachers not *for* the teachers—which contributed to the overall meaning and satisfaction with the trainings. Based on this learning from the FPP, teachers should have more influence in selecting professional learning designs to meet both their and their students' needs.

HOW CAN LEARNING DESIGNS BE CONNECTED TO THE TEACHER EVALUATION SYSTEM?

During the first year of implementation of the FPP, teachers selected a learning design based on interest, passion, learning with other teachers, and a desire for greater support for students. To start the second year, a valid question is, How can the reasons for selecting learning designs be expanded to include a more thorough analysis of student and teacher learning needs, connect more deeply to teacher evaluation domain elements, and provide a clearer articulation of individual and team goals—without making the process so detailed that teachers lose their excitement and passion for choice? How can the selection of learning designs use both teacher affect—the psychological/emotional and social dimensions—as well as data—the technical dimension—to support areas of need? (See Chapter 7.) Beginning the second year, teachers will be offered a checklist to select learning designs to better understand the intended purpose and learning outcomes of the design, and to tightly align learning with developing effectiveness with the Five Agreements and areas of student need.

Checklist for Teachers: Selecting Your Learning Design

1. What do the student and teacher evaluation data indicate?

   o Locate and analyze student and teacher evaluation data.

2. What are your and your students' learning needs?

   o Identify the educator and student learning needs.

3. What is the new idea or practice to develop or understand more deeply?

   o Identify the new idea or practice to develop a more complete understanding.

4. What are the types of learning designs and their purpose?

   o Read the descriptors of the learning designs.

5. What is the intended outcome of actively engaging in the learning design?

   o Identify intended outcome of the design based on educator and student needs.

6. Which learning design is the most appropriate for you to develop effectiveness with the Five Practices?

   o Identify 1 to 5 of the agreed-on Five Agreements to become more effective.

7. What is the most appropriate learning design for both your and students' needs?

   o Read descriptors of the different learning designs.

8. Which learning design most interests you?

   o Select a learning design.

There are some concerns about teachers' use of the checklist. Will selecting a learning design become too technical? Alternatively, will teachers see the checklist as an enhancement to selecting a learning design for their professional learning? Will the checklist contribute to the psychological/emotional dimensions of their professional learning that they valued this year? It seems that the checklist could be an appropriate tool for teachers to use for selecting learning designs that deepen knowledge of their practice and continue to address the three dimensions of professional learning that meet both educator and student needs.

WHAT HAPPENS WHEN TEACHERS
HAVE A VOICE IN SELECTING LEARNING DESIGNS?

When teachers have a voice in selecting learning designs, they are cognitively, psychologically, and socially invested in their learning. Teachers do value choice in selecting learning designs as evidenced by the thoughtful and creative ways they shared their learning and student results at the Knowledge Showcase. Each design team spent time, effort, and energy preparing a way to share their learning with whole school staff from their active engagement in Cycles 1 and 2. Because there wasn't a prescribed way to share, each team used a different method that reflected their unique style and creativity. For example, teachers created PowerPoint presentations, which included video clips of the students in action, samples of student work, and teachers in action. Teachers shared student work samples and data charts from short-cycle assessments showing increases in student learning. Many teachers claimed that their learning from Part 3 of the FPP was a contributing factor for student achievement. Most of the Knowledge Showcase sessions were so powerful that I felt that I was at a national conference engaged in an informative session.

Teachers say . . .

- "We had fun with Video Study with Application. We finally had a chance to study new ways to teach counting and cardinality by watching videos and trying the strategies out. We were inspired by videos we had seen earlier and wanted a chance to look for successful approaches."
- "Our dual language fifth-grade team finally enjoyed learning in each others classrooms. We selected the Collaborative Teaching and Assessing because our students struggle with coordinate pairs, and we all have different results with this topic. We could focus on this topic and found out that we all teach the concept differently. Our students scored better on tasks about coordinate grids on the end of year assessment."
- "We enjoyed Lesson Design. It was hard work but the learning was so great for all of us."
- "I *loved* having time to learn from a project I have always been passionate about and include other people with me."

What was powerful were the words teachers used to describe their professional learning experience—*inspirational, loved, hard work, learning, enjoyment, fun, successful*—words that are not often used by teachers in the context of high-stakes accountability. In some circles, scholars, administrators, and educators would describe the words teachers used as *fluffy*, *fuzzy*, or *feel good*, implying a lack of substance and results. Rather than *fluffy*, might the words *actively engaged*, *motivated*, *effective*, *successful*, and *empowered* be used to describe the teachers' experiences? After all, most teachers did produce quantitative student data showing gains in student achievement that aligned with their investment in learning. Can we acknowledge that the affective descriptors measuring teacher self-efficacy and optimal experience correlate alongside the same data-driven world in the context of accountability?

An important learning from implementing the FPP is that stronger coherence must exist between the learning design, its purpose, and a stated, explicit connection to the Five Agreements aligned with teacher evaluation domains. An educator "working language" promoting coherence would include verbal connections to the design goal, activities, what is being learned, the Five Agreements, and teacher evaluation elements. Here's what a working language of coherence would sound like: A teacher asks the question—how will learning "this" help us learn to (name 1 of the five practices)? Examples: How can studying classroom discussions strategies increase student engagement? What types of questions are effective in increasing the level of cognitive demand? Where does our lesson plan design include student-to-student questioning?

Teachers need more information for selecting designs such as the design descriptor and checklist, and more time to make a thoughtful selection. Teachers chose designs in one hour. When selecting designs, I recommend at least two hours of thoughtful reflection about a choice that will last an entire year.

During Year 2, what could be done differently?

- Use a checklist for selecting designs.
- Create a stronger support system in place for implementation, meaning a coach or teacher leader participates in all phases of the design cycle—planning/implementation/assessing, reflecting—and follow up with feedback and questions that push thinking and create coherence.
- Study the teacher evaluation domain and elements in more depth.
- Identify the new idea or practice to develop a more complete understanding.
- Use student data more often for instructional decision making.

YOUR TURN—START THE CONVERSATION

1. How are learning designs currently selected in your district or at your schools?

2. Who selects learning designs for teacher participation and learning? To what degree do teachers have a voice in choosing learning designs?

3. How are learning designs aligned with your state's teacher evaluation system?

4. How has your school created a collaborative—not competitive—environment that supports professional learning?

5. How much time do teachers spend collaborating for learning? Calculate the time teachers have for professional learning at your school. In one hour, how many minutes are used for data analysis and what to do with the data? How do teachers spend time collaborating for learning? How much time do teachers spend analyzing data? How much time do teachers spend learning what do differently after analyzing the data? What do you notice?

6. If you were to pick five teachers randomly at your school and ask them the question, "Where, when, and how are you learning to improve your practice based on the teacher evaluation system?" what would they say and what would you hear?

Assessing and Evaluating Changes

5

"Not all evaluation of professional learning requires rigorous, academic evaluation. On the contrary, when professional learning is focused on changing educator practice and improving student outcomes, all educators have the ability—and the responsibility—to gather evidence and participate in the evaluation of professional learning as part of a system of continuous improvement."

—Learning Forward (2012)

"What changed for us is that we learned how to design activities using technology that increased student engagement and questioning skills."

—Vertical Technology Design Team, Hamos Elementary

"We learned how to set up and manage group work and facilitate a segment of instruction so students developed a better understanding of the distributive property."

—Lesson Design Team, Terra Elementary

In this chapter, the following questions are addressed:

- What is the difference between assessment and evaluation, and why is this important?

- What was assessed during implementation of the Five-Part Plan (FPP)?
- What changed as a result of teachers actively engaging in the FPP?
- What is a doable, manageable process you can use to assess changes during implementation of the FPP?

At the end of this chapter, you will be able to

- distinguish the difference between assessment and evaluation and reasons for considering the difference;
- identify what was assessed and evaluated during implementation of the FPP;
- name what changes resulted from implementation of the FPP; and
- identify a checklist you can use for assessing and evaluating changes as a result of teachers actively engaging in the FPP.

ASSESSING TEACHER EVALUATION

It was mid-May when a principal, two teacher leaders, and I developed the FPP in the principal's office. You may recall in Chapter 1 of this book that the need for a strategy arose when the principal described a bleak, overwhelming situation. "We are implementing a new teacher evaluation system and new curriculum resources with little to no time for teachers to engage in professional learning." The question we struggled to answer was, How can teachers possibly prepare for the teacher evaluation system during their 180 days, forty hours per week of time spent on a school campus? The day after this conversation, I emailed an outline of the FPP for the principal to consider as a formalized plan to designate time for teachers to engage in *meaningful* professional learning. This included the co-creation of a shared vision, selection of learning designs, active engagement in two cycles of the learning design, sharing knowledge at the end of the year, and archiving knowledge to remember. If the FPP was started in August, what changes in teacher knowledge, skills, and dispositions could we expect by May, and would there be time to observe any measureable student results? Would educators value learning from the FPP, and would they want to continue it the following year? There was an obvious need for some type of assessment and evaluation of the FPP. What kind? How do we want to evaluate or assess changes? Moreover, how do busy school-based educators find the time to assess the value and impact of their professional learning plan? These questions are addressed in this chapter.

During a conference roundtable discussion . . . With educators who were learning about how to apply for grant monies, I was introduced as the "evaluator" and asked to talk about the process used to evaluate all grant awardees. I asked the future grant applicants, "When you hear the word *evaluation*, what words come to mind?" As one might expect, grimaces and body language hinted that nobody liked to be subjected to evaluation, and the group's verbal responses confirmed that this was an area of anxiety. Some were "afraid of the money being taken back," or "afraid to be judged," and others thought they might be exposed for "not knowing how to do it right." Of course, the intention of awarding the grant was to support awardees growth and professional learning and to learn from their experiences, not to create an episode on *Fear Factor*. However, evaluation is necessary for determining the value of investing money in a grant.

During conversations with teachers . . . I posed the question, "How do you feel about the new teacher evaluation system?" Teachers shared similar concerns and anxieties as the grant applicants during the roundtable discussion—"nervous," "it's a gotcha," "anxious about getting an effective rating," and so on. Another commenter added, "It depends on the principal and how she uses the observation data."

During a planning conversation with a colleague . . . When our professional learning team was planning an experience for math teachers, a colleague asserted, "We need everyone to know how this project is evaluated." Another colleague cautioned, "Let's *don't* send a message of evaluation to teachers. We don't want to them to think they are now being evaluated by *us* along with the state's teacher evaluation system."

Because language matters, the decision was made in August (1) to assess—not evaluate—changes and improvements which occurred because teachers participated in the FPP and (2) to identify what teachers found valuable and meaningful through active engagement in two cycles of learning designs.

WHAT IS THE DIFFERENCE BETWEEN ASSESSMENT AND EVALUATION, AND WHY IS THIS IMPORTANT?

Assessment seems to be a "friendlier" and more receptive word than *evaluation*, evoking less stressful responses from people. It may seem at first like a small difference in semantics, but words, when chosen thoughtfully, can create a big difference in attitudes. Assessment can either be *formative*—providing useful feedback for the improvement of teaching and learning—or *summative*—another word for evaluation, meaning that final and perhaps ominous measure of quality. Assessment can be defined as a process that focuses on learning that involves reviewing and reflecting on practice in a planned and careful way (Palomba & Banta, 1999, p. 1).

Evaluation is the process of observing and measuring a thing for the purpose of judging it and of determining its "value," either by comparison to similar things, or to a standard. Evaluation of teaching means passing judgment on actions and behavior as part of a way to measure teacher effectiveness. Evaluation can be defined as the "systematic process of determining the merit, value, and worth of someone (the evaluee, such as a teacher, student, or employee) or something (the evaluand, such as a product, program, policy, procedure, or process)" ("Evaluation glossary," 2007). Assessment and evaluation differ not only in their purposes but also in their use of collected information. While it is possible to use the same tools for the two approaches, the use of the data collected differs. For example, a principal can use the results of a teacher observation for both assessment and evaluation purposes. The results can be used to provide feedback to the teacher to strengthen student learning or to decide what rating to give each teacher, that is, to judge teacher effectiveness using ratings on a continuum from ineffective to exemplary.

Distinguishing the difference between assessment and evaluation of the FPP is important for three reasons. Using the term *assessment* created three perceptions: (1) My role on the FPP was the data gatherer and learning partner—not researcher or evaluator, which may have contributed to educators sharing information in more honest and open ways. (2) The teacher, coach, and principal could safely learn alongside each other without judgment. They were on the same team and sharing the same goals for supporting "our" students' learning. As a principal put it, "I could take off my evaluator hat and participate in the learning designs." (3) The FPP was a process separate from, yet correlated with, teacher evaluation where teachers found psychological safety, a less anxious and stressful learning space where new methods of teaching were assessed, not teachers evaluated. By assessing rather than evaluating, the FPP promoted growth and optimal learning experiences by enabling teachers to learn and practice their skills in a "flow" situation—where mistakes are valued opportunities to improve. How was assessment connected to evaluation? Learning that occurred during engagement in lesson design cycles was intended to support changes in classroom practices as measured by teacher evaluation observations. The decision to assess the FPP, yet disconnect it from teacher evaluation, provided teachers an opportunity to engage in professional learning in a climate of collaboration and trust. Only when a school separates the teacher evaluation space from the FPP learning design space will a climate of collaboration, trust, and inquiry emerge.

Language is important. The terms *researcher* and *evaluator* imply distance, hierarchy, and judgment. A *learning partner* implies a more egalitarian approach for a two-way exchange of information. If educators freely share information, we are in a better position to learn together. If teachers fear being evaluated and judged, they are more likely to withhold information, self-protect, and block open exchange of information. As a learning partner, when I ask teachers, instructional coaches, and principals for interviews, to write reflections, or to share artifacts with me such as video and PowerPoint slides, they accept willingly. Educators' availability, accessibility, and willingness to share and to receive feedback was partly due to their perception of my role as a fellow professional learner being curious and helpful. In other words, they trusted me as someone wanting to learn alongside them and support their growth.

The FPP process should create a safe space for learning in collaboration resulting in growth—not a place where teachers are judged as to their worthiness. Since the word *evaluation* is linked to the new teacher evaluation, already generating angst for both principals and teachers, the word *assessment* is preferred to more accurately describe a process for gathering evidence for learning how the FPP is making a difference.

WHAT IS ASSESSED DURING IMPLEMENTATION OF THE FIVE-PART PLAN, AND HOW IS IT ASSESSED?

Two target areas for assessment are changes in teacher practice linked to student learning, and the value of the FPP as a structure for active engagement in professional learning. Questions for assessment and learning include the following:

- What changes did teachers make as a result of participating in the lesson design cycles?
- What changes did students make?
- What did teachers find valuable and meaningful in the experience?
- Would you want to engage in the FPP next year? If yes, how would you change it?

Data were gathered in August, January, and May from interviews with principals, teachers, and instructional coaches, written reflections, emails, student artifacts, and site visits. Unfortunately, the students were not interviewed. It would be a great source of information to interview students after the teachers engaged in the lesson implementation part of the lesson design cycle! What did students learn as a result of their teachers planning for the lesson students just experienced? What did students enjoy/not enjoy about the lesson? What would they change? Student feedback could be used to inform revisions to the lesson.

Guskey's *Evaluating Professional Development* (2000) informed the questions used during assessment. Educators' responses were interpreted through three dimensions of professional learning—technical, psychological, and social (see Chapter 7). Questions considered for each dimension included the following:

- Technical—did you have enough time, resources to engage in the cycles, and was the FPP doable and manageable in the fast paced life of schooling?
- Psychological/Emotional—did you find the learning meaningful?
- Social—what did you find valuable about collaborations with other teachers?

(See Chapter 9 for what was learned.)

WHAT CHANGES OR IMPROVEMENTS WERE MADE BY TEACHERS WHO ACTIVELY ENGAGED IN THE FIVE-PART PLAN?

Principals, teachers, and instructional coaches saw positive changes as a result of implementing the FPP. Most educators agreed that a focus on the Five Agreements (Part 1 of the FPP), initiated by teachers, self-selection of and engagement in the learning designs, were contributing factors for enhancing change. However, a cause-and-effect result cannot be claimed.

What changed for teachers? They had time and place for learning collaboratively, and choice in the selection of the learning design that they would not have had without the FPP. The primary reason for the creation and design of the FPP was to address the need for teachers to have time and structure for job-embedded professional learning. Teachers in the four schools had time to meet in professional learning communities (PLCs) or in other team meetings. However, in three of the four schools, this time was used for sharing logistical information and data analysis exclusively. Chavez High School was the exception. Their PLC was a place for learning and was used to reflect and learn what they could do to support students. Other changes for teachers as a result of participation in the FPP included new grouping strategies to allow more students opportunities to engage with the content, using formative assessment strategies more often, using strategies for increasing student-to-student engagement, greater use of technology with student involvement, personal and professional enjoyment through collaboration with other teachers, and their personal choice in selecting learning designs.

Teachers say . . .

"Through our increased collaboration, connecting, and reviewing the project in academic areas, students had the opportunity to practice skills and verbalize learning to show understanding."

"We learned how to design SMART Board activities so students could interact and learn from each other by questioning one another and sharing their thinking."

"We learned how to increase student engagement. It took practice and then we finally became comfortable, feeling successful ourselves."

What changed for principals and instructional coaches? Principals found the FPP helpful for evaluating teachers on the teacher evaluation "professionalism" domain, as they had evidence of active engagement in the Learning Design Cycles, written reflections, and participation in the Knowledge Showcase. Principals and instructional coaches also found a place to learn alongside teachers during implementation of the learning designs. Principals, teachers, and instructional coaches shared a common language about the Five Agreements—practices that should be in every classroom every day. Four principals indicated the FPP promoted effectiveness in teacher professionalism aligned to the teacher evaluation domain, and had evidence that "made it easier" to rate teachers as effective, highly effective, or exemplary. Instructional coaches found an increase in positive teacher collaboration as teachers worked in partnership toward shared goals.

Principals say . . .

"We gave teachers the power to realize they have what it takes to change what they do and make a difference for students. They created ownership of their learning and held themselves accountable for student results."

"Its great to see you guys own your own professional learning, and even more exciting to see the impact on student learning."

Instructional coaches say . . .

"Teachers developed the confidence to create activities themselves, and to support each other in engaging students."

"The teachers enjoyed studying video and learned how to make the activities come alive for students. They made the activities, like 'Making Ten' even better."

What changed for students? Principal and teacher observations, videos, student artifacts, and short-cycle assessment data provide evidence that students increased their engagement with technology, engagement with each other, use of content vocabulary, mathematics procedural and conceptual understanding in geometry, fluency with number and in algebraic thinking, and literacy skills, and increased the frequency and ability to question each other. Students were not interviewed, and on later reflection, I realized this was a missed opportunity and should be added to the FPP assessment process to give a more systemic picture of change using multiple perspectives.

Assessment Questions

- What changes did you make as a result of participating in the lesson design cycles?
- What changes did students make?
- What did you value about engaging in the FPP?
- Would you want to engage in the FPP next year? If yes, how would you change it?

WHAT IS A "DOABLE," MANAGEABLE PROCESS YOU CAN USE TO ASSESS IMPROVEMENTS DURING IMPLEMENTATION OF THE FIVE-PART PLAN?

Research and experts in the field agree that an essential part of the school improvement process is documenting, monitoring, and collecting evidence (Hargreaves & Fullan, 2012; Reeves, 2010). However, it's difficult for busy practitioners to find time for assessing the value and meaning of educator professional learning and its impact on students. School-based educators juggle a multitude of tasks and initiatives while keeping the students and staff safe from harm. Keeping all the plates spinning and balanced is quite an accomplishment. If you were to ask school-based educators to assess the impact of their professional learning on changes in student achievement, most would throw their hands up in frustration and say, "That is just *one* more thing to do!" How can the FPP be assessed in this "too busy" context? Let's consider why busy practitioners should assess school based professional learning, specifically the FPP, and how to assess using a checklist to keep track.

Question: What is the benefit to staff and students if educators assess their school's professional learning plan?

Answer: You assess to determine whether changes in teaching and learning are occurring, and whether or not those changes are improving

Table 5.1 Responses to Assessment Questions for the Five-Part Plan

	Chavez High School	Hamos Elementary	Gainfield Elementary	Terra Elementary
1. What changes did teachers make as a result of participating in the lesson design cycles?	• Use of formative assessment using "My Favorite No" • Created common ground • Asking more higher level questions • More collaboration and team teaching • Shifted from direct teaching to facilitated learning • Using "how-to vocabulary"	• Use of technology • Increased vertical collaboration • Increased student-to-student engagement • Used appropriate content vocabulary • Used learning targets and criteria for success • Created a respectful learning environment	• Using a variety of formative assessment strategies • Increased collaboration • Shared focus	• Increased use of strategies for classroom discourse • Use of content vocabulary • Used intentional strategies for increase student collaboration • Sequenced lessons for greater access for all students
2. What changes did students make?	• Increased engagement • Use of mathematics vocabulary in small group discussions • Use of peer feedback • Working in groups • Posted their student work publicly	• Asked each other questions • Used content vocabulary more often when talking with each other • Used more respectful behaviors • Increased ability to work in groups	• No data	• Increased active engagement in learning and with each other • Increased use of content vocabulary • Respected each other with language and behavior

(Continued)

Table 5.1 (Continued)

	Chavez High School	Hamos Elementary	Gainfield Elementary	Terra Elementary
3. What did you value about engaging in the FPP?	• Time for collaboration • Opportunity to teach with another teacher • Shared focus • Five Agreements • Opportunity to select learning design	• Vertical connections • Ability to select and own the work	• Enjoyment in learning collaboratively • Selecting our own learning design	• Time to collaborate • Planning and teaching in each other's classrooms • Shared focus on five goals • Clear "how-to" structure
4. Would you want to participate in the FPP next year? How would you change it?	78% Yes Change: • Greater alignment to school goals • Participate on voluntary basis	100% Yes Change: • With our move to turnaround school and new principal, let's just keep doing it	No data	100% Yes Change: • Whole school vertical connection

student learning. You also assess to know why your data are increasing, staying the same, or decreasing. You can determine whether teachers have time to learn what to teach differently, and what support is needed to get different results from the data.

If you use the FPP to design your school for meaningful professional learning, it has a manageable, well-defined method to assess value and growth, despite the fast-paced life of schooling. Each teacher uses the one-page chart to record information and store it electronically (see Table 5.2); at the end of the year, each teacher has a record of growth and change in practice resulting from engaging in the cycles of learning designs. The teacher and principal can use the record as evidence to inform the measure level of effectiveness on teacher evaluation domain "professionalism," and the instructional coach and teacher can use the document for ongoing reflection in practice learning conversations. Using this one-page table will allow principals to determine whether teachers have the time, a place, and a structure for continuous professional learning throughout the school year. It also helps principals to determine if teachers find the professional learning experiences meaningful for improving student learning.

1. Do you have time, resources, and support to engage in the Learning Design Cycles?

2. What are you learning? Why?

Table 5.2 Assessment of Professional Learning

Questions	August	After Design Cycle 1	After Design Cycle 2	May
1. Do you have time resources and support to engage in the Learning Design Cycles?	Needed:	Needed:	Needed:	
2. What are you learning? Why?		Evidence:	Evidence:	Evidence:
3. What changes are you making?		Evidence:	Evidence:	Evidence:
4. What changes are students making?		Evidence:	Evidence:	Evidence:
5. What do you value about the learning experience?				

3. What changes are you making?

4. What changes are students making?

5. What did you value about the learning experience?

The Principal   6

The Key to Making Learning
Happen

"The learning leader is the one who models learning and shapes the
conditions for all to learn on a continual basis."

—Michael Fullan

"The 'big picture' is that teachers collaborate using reflective practice
in a rich, meaningful way with choice in their learning, leading to
changes in instruction and improved student learning."

—Mashelle, high school assistant principal

"You have to draw on innate teachers passion and abilities and
beliefs. Teachers need to be encouraged to develop on a positive note."

—Maria, elementary school principal

In this chapter, the following questions are addressed:

- What was the principal's role in successful implementation of the Five-Part Plan (FPP)?
- What essential understandings did the principals have to implement the FPP?
- What and how were the supportive conditions created for implementing the FPP?

- How did principals facilitate conversations that provided constructive feedback for change?

At the end of this chapter, you will be able to

- identify actions taken by the principal to support successful implementation of the FPP;
- develop awareness of the principal's essential understandings to implement the FPP;
- identify the supportive conditions necessary for successful implementation of the FPP; and
- determine facilitation strategies that create conversations that promote constructive feedback.

INTRODUCING THE FIVE-PART PLAN TO LEADERS

The FPP was co-created synergistically with a principal, two teacher leaders, and a university partner to systemically design a school for professional learning. It was then formally introduced to twenty-six administrators during a summer leadership academy.

FPP for Designing Your School for Professional Learning

Part 1—Reaching Consensus

What five things should be in every classroom every day?

Part 2—Selecting the Learning Design

How do teachers learn to do those five things effectively?

Part 3—Implementing the Learning Design Cycle

What is a Learning Design Cycle, and how is it implemented?

Part 4—Sharing Professional Knowledge with Whole School Staff

What is a Knowledge Showcase?

Part 5—Creating a Professional Knowledge Base

How does a school archive learning so it is not lost?

During the summer academy, principals, assistant superintendents, district-level administrators, and teacher leaders were introduced to protocols for FPP enactment and shown how to create a timeline for implementation.

By the end of the session, I offered interested schools ongoing support if they decided to implement the FPP. This would include my facilitating sessions at their school site and documenting evidence of progress as part of the improvement process. Of the twenty-two in attendance, nine principals in four districts expressed interest and wanted more information about how to implement the FPP. I scheduled brief meetings with each principal, teacher leader, and instructional coach in their school to discuss logistics for implementation. Logistics included setting a date before the first day of school to facilitate Parts 1 and 2—creating Five Agreements with staff about what practices should be in every classroom, every day, aligning the practices with the teacher evaluation rubric, signing up for their professional learning design (PLD) of choice, and identifying dates to implement Cycle 1 of the PLD (see Chapter 2). After the thirty-minute meetings, all nine principals were still interested in implementing the FPP.

Later that summer, principals attended required "training" on the new state teacher evaluation system to learn requirements for conducting teacher observations and documenting observations using technology. The new system proved demanding both in time and energy. It would be challenging to implement, and required that principals make frequent classroom observations to be recorded on a computer database. After attending the summer sessions, five of the nine principals decided to delay implementation of the FPP, explaining that it was "just too much" this year and "something else" on their plates. Even the reluctant principals, however, still wanted to revisit the FPP later. "Maybe [we can] implement next year after we get the new Teacher Evaluation system going."

In contrast to the five principals dropping the FPP, however, four of the nine principals—three elementary principals and one high school assistant principal—still wanted to implement the FPP in the upcoming school year. What did the principals "get," specifically, that convinced them to go forward, in spite of distracting initiatives? What were their essential understandings, and what was the "how-to" practitioner knowledge that equipped principals to implement the FPP?

WHAT WAS THE PRINCIPAL'S ROLE IN SUCCESSFUL IMPLEMENTATION OF THE FIVE-PART PLAN?

"Getting it" means that the principal understands two fundamental ideas:

Idea 1—"the big picture"—the purpose and benefits of professional learning, the vision for building a school culture that nurtures professional learning, and knows how to create that vision with all staff members

Idea 2—the "how-to," specifically, knowing

- the logistics for implementation;
- how to create supportive conditions to promote growth and development of professionals within their schools;
- how to facilitate conversations that provide constructive feedback for change; and
- how to collect and use data as evidence of progress.

Principals' responsibilities are demanding in the high-stakes context of accountability. Principals are expected to manage a school safely and efficiently, serve as an instructional leader, implement new initiatives, adhere to Common Core Standards, direct teacher evaluation and state assessments, attend mandated trainings, connect with parents and the community, support teachers' growth, and get results. The current state of "principaling" is too much to do coupled with too little time. How can a principal's focus be on supporting teachers' professional learning when there are so many day-to-day demands? What was it about the FPP that appealed to the four principals?

WHAT ESSENTIAL UNDERSTANDINGS DID THE PRINCIPALS HAVE TO IMPLEMENT THE FIVE-PART PLAN?

The principals who decided to implement the FPP demonstrated three essential understandings. First, they understood the fundamental importance of creating a school culture that values professional learning as the primary mechanism for teachers to improve student learning. Second, each principal valued co-creating and sharing the vision with all staff members, so the FPP was jointly owned and not just another "mandate from above." Third, the principals valued empowering teachers with choice in decision making and supporting their growth. When the principals first heard about the FPP, some were already looking for something similar. One principal, Krista, exclaimed, "This is just what I needed!" She realized the FPP gave the principals the "know-how" to structure the school year so teachers had time for professional learning, and provided voice and choice in choosing learning designs that fit both teachers' and students' growth place. Principals also saw the FPP as a support system for the teacher evaluation system, and dovetailed with it in a way so teachers could respond constructively to its demands. The FPP provided a structure, time, and learning space for teachers to become more effective as measured through the teacher evaluation process. Ray, principal of one of the elementary schools, said,

The "big picture" that I saw had to do with our school and two main changes [that were needed]. The first being a need to increase student achievement and for improving our letter grade that dropped to a "D." The second being a need to make sure there was a strong professional development component in place to meet the requirements set forth in the new teacher evaluation system.

The four principals who did not delay the FPP perceived it as a logical response piece to teacher evaluation. This view of the FPP as a much-needed "solution," as opposed to "one more thing," would soon lead the four principals to implement opportunities for teachers to improve *and* be involved in the improvement process.

Each principal introduced the FPP and fully participated in creating the vision with all staff members so it was jointly owned. Before the first day of school, principals scheduled two hours with whole school staff and announced that "we have an opportunity to get on the same page with what our classrooms should look like every day" and a plan for "learning how to be effective at creating these classrooms. How do we do this together?" Principals who got it shared the belief that implementing the FPP was not something extra. Instead, they perceived the FPP as a necessary organizing structure for promoting effective teaching as measured by the state's teacher evaluation rubric.

WHAT WERE THE SUPPORTIVE CONDITIONS FOR IMPLEMENTING THE FIVE-PART PLAN, AND HOW WERE THE CONDITIONS CREATED?

Supportive conditions refers to the physical conditions and professional relationships for how a staff finds time to learn together, has voice and choice in decision making, and engages in creative work that educators find optimal (Csikszentmihalyi, 1997; SEDL, 1997). Schools that successfully implemented the FPP had the following structures in place: time to meet and talk (whole school staff professional learning sessions/meetings, weekly collaboration time), well-developed communication structures (morning messages, weekly e-mails for teachers to hear about the plan, information about upcoming events), and schedules and resources for collaboration (substitute teachers, teaching assistants).

The FPP helps to create supportive conditions at schools by providing the implementation plan. This includes the timeline for implementation, professional learning designs that align with the requirements as part of Domain 4—professionalism—of the teacher evaluation process, and

serves as the space where teachers grow their knowledge and skills in Domains 2 and 3—learning environment and instruction.

Drawing from the literature and research world, we know that the principal must repeatedly communicate the vision during the school year in whole group faculty meetings, in small group learning teams, in conversations with individual teachers, and with parents and the broader community. These continual reminders act as support for how curricular, instructional, and assessment decisions are made both inside and outside the classroom. The effective principal uses "words that encourage" (Eisenbach, 2014) that support teacher morale through the "difficult middle"—the time period when excitement has waned and vacation seems far in the distance.

How were the supportive conditions created? After the initial rollout of Parts 1 and 2, the principal's role is to keep the vision alive with continual, encouraging reminders about the Five Agreements and important dates for the upcoming cycle. The principal also makes sure substitute teachers are available when the teacher participates in their chosen PLD.

Here is what supportive conditions look like in action.

Maria, an elementary principal, supported implementation of Cycle 1 (plan for one hour, implement the lesson for one hour, reflect on student learning for one hour) of the FPP by scheduling one day in mid-September for teacher teams to reflect with external partners on the progress of their PLD. Prior to the reflection sessions, Maria e-mailed every teacher a schedule with meeting times for each PLD team and names of teachers on each team. She ended the message with, "I'm really excited about this opportunity and can hardly wait to see what the teams will be learning!" Six PLD teams—Video Study, Technology, Lesson Design, Creative and Innovative Teaching, and Vertical Team Study (two teams)—met with the principal and external partners for thirty minutes each between 8:55 and 2:10. In the meeting room, the Five Agreements of what should be in every classroom every day was posted. SMART Boards displayed plans, lessons, and videos of lessons and students as evidence of progress toward their goals. Teachers shared, asked questions, and linked their learning to the Five Agreements.

Teachers were galvanized by their inclusion in creating the Five Agreements . . .

"All of these ideas start coming . . . as we learn with each other."

"I feel that I have the power to be effective."

"I'm excited—I love working with all these ladies, and it's been a while since I've been in other teachers' classrooms."

"I never thought I would have the opportunity to create my own project. I'm learning how students can integrate graphing, social studies, language arts, and writing."

Maria's insights about the session included, "This plan is giving teachers the power to realize they have what it takes to be effective."

Krista, an elementary principal, supported teachers through implementation of Cycle 1 of the FPP by using one of two whole staff monthly meetings to plan for the upcoming PLD cycle. Prior to the meeting, Krista sent an e-mail to the staff clearly stating the purpose for the meeting (meet with teams to plan for Cycle 1 of the PLD) and reflected on progress so far. Krista facilitated the meeting with the external partner (the author, in this case) present to listen to successes and concerns, to connect teams' actions to the Five Agreements, and to document teachers' comments. During the meeting, Krista continually provided encouragement to motivate teachers to learn and create. She emphasized to teachers that she "knows they can succeed," and linked their work with the Five Agreements and teacher evaluation.

Both principals provided the following supportive conditions:

- Time to meet, talk, and learn—Principals initiate meeting logistics. Meeting dates are put on the calendar, time is scheduled to reflect, address concerns, and share evidence of process. Substitute teachers are provided, external partners invited. Each principal encouraged collaboration and ensured that teachers developed the capacity, knowledge, and skills to engage in productive discourse.
- Well-developed communication structures—Principals created a schedule of meeting times, communicated a purpose for each meeting, and shared expectations for participation. Written reminders were sent one week prior to the scheduled meetings.
- Teachers have voice and choice in decision making—Each teacher chose a PLD and had voice in identifying the Five Agreements of what teacher and student behaviors and practices should be in every classroom every day.

HOW DID PRINCIPALS FACILITATE CONVERSATIONS THAT PROVIDED CONSTRUCTIVE FEEDBACK FOR CHANGE?

Feedback is an essential element for everyone in a school, but it must be constructive to achieve the desired results. The objective in giving feedback is to provide guidance by supplying information in a useful manner either to support effective practices or to guide someone toward effectiveness. Feedback is constructive when there is a clear purpose for giving feedback; it is based on observed behavior, withholds judgment, and can be reciprocal, as it allows the other person to respond. Feedback is a critical tool for knowing when things are moving in the direction toward one's goals. Constructive feedback is *nonjudgmental* communication that alerts a person to a specific area in which his/her performance could improve. This positive form of feedback helps principals and staff to pinpoint incremental improvements, while also acknowledging teachers for results already obtained from intentional, purposeful continuous learning. Constructive feedback occurs during one-on-one, ongoing performance discussions, during coaching situations, and also in teams that are implementing a common lesson. Constructive feedback also occurs when someone asks for your opinion about how the person is doing or as part of teacher performance as measured by the teacher evaluation system.

Constructive feedback can sound as follows:

1. Stating the purpose

   "I have some thoughts about . . ."
   "I want to discuss . . ."

2. Describing an observation

   "I observed fifteen students out of twenty-four students interacting with each other during the math task. I noticed that nine students were not talking and working alone."

3. Giving the other person a chance to respond

   "What is your view of the situation?"

4. Thinking together about solutions

   "What are some additional strategies to engage more students?"

5. Summarizing and checking on progress

   "Since student engagement is what we are all working toward as part of our shared agreements, it may be useful to try the *Think, Pair, Share* strategy and observe the results. Let's talk for five minutes next week or e-mail me to reflect on this question: Did the *Think, Pair, Share* strategy increase students engagement in the math task? Let me know what support you need to implement this strategy."

6. Providing encouraging words

   "I want to acknowledge your willingness to try something new to support all students' engagement in their learning."

Principals had four tools to draw on for providing constructive feedback: *Building Rapport, Skills for Managing Respectful Conflict* (Benjamin, Yeager, & Simon, 2012), *Concerns-Based Adoption Model* (Hall & Hord, 2015), and the book *Adaptive School* (Garmston & Wellman, 2013). These tools were shared with principals during leadership academy learning sessions, which occurred five times during the school year.

1. Building Rapport

> Mirror body language—gestures
> Mimic tonality—volume
> Breathe like they breathe
> Match their rate of speech
> Paraphrase and approve
> Assume you already have rapport

The principals were shown the six skills for building rapport. The facilitator modeled the process by building rapport with a principal she did not know very well. Each principal then practiced building rapport with another principal in the room they did not know well. They were asked to try building rapport at the beginning of the year prior to teacher evaluation to make it "safe" for the teacher to hear and benefit from constructive feedback.

Principals were asked to reflect on building rapport at the next principals learning academy.

2. Skills for Managing Respectful Conflict

We drew on the work of Benjamin et al. (2012) to identify and build skills for transferring information in conversation. We studied "Yes, but" comments, which are defined as words that send a mixed message because they contain two ideas—an agreement and a competing idea. According to Benjamin et al., "Yes, buts" can fuel an argument and instead of providing constructive feedback can result in destructive anger and anxiety. Principals built their knowledge of using "Yes, buts," then practiced using them in a feedback simulation with a teacher.

Example: Principal says, "Your students were engaged as they were interacting with each other, but I don't know that they were interacting with the math task enough."

What the teacher heard was that "I don't know that they were interacting with the math task enough."

After developing awareness of "Yes, buts," the principals then explored skills for managing them. Are principals aware of using "Yes, buts" in feedback situations?

For example, a teacher states, "I'm so frustrated, I don't know what to pay attention to anymore. Do I pay attention to the short-cycle data, Common Core Standards, or my textbook? What decisions do I make?" The principal listens and attentively and asks, "Can you think of a way to address this issue?" Principals practiced using listening and asking questions, and were encouraged to use this strategy during feedback sessions.

3. Concerns Based Adoption Model (CBAM)

Principals were encouraged to use the concerns model to listen to teachers and identify their level of concern. The concerns-based model identifies and provides ways to assess seven stages of concern, which have implications for providing feedback as principals identify the stage of concern of the teacher. Knowing the stage of concern allows the principal to provide feedback that addresses questions, comments, and concerns of the teachers. What kind of feedback could be used to move teachers to a growth place?

Situation: A first year teacher has a poor evaluation. She starts crying in the follow-up conference. The principal recognizes that the teacher has personal concerns and responds with an appropriate verbal intervention for the teacher's stage of concern. The principal states, "I know you are capable of effective teaching and I want to encourage you to try again. Let's talk about what worked and didn't work in the lesson and create a learning place for you to learn what to do to get an effective rating."

4. Adaptive School

Principals received a copy of the Garmston and Wellman (2013) book, which describes tools, strategies, and processes for creating situations where constructive feedback could be received safely and used effectively to achieve the desired results.

YOUR TURN—START THE CONVERSATION

1. How is your school designed so teachers have ongoing professional learning connected to their classroom during the school year?

2. What "big picture" do you have for designing your school for professional learning?

3. What supportive conditions currently exist in your school that promote growth and development?

4. How do you facilitate conversations that provide constructive feed-back for change?

5. What data are you currently using to assess the impact of teacher professional learning during the school year? Do teachers apply their new learning in the classroom and, if so, to what extent?

6. What understanding do principals in your district need to implement the FPP at school sites?

Three Dimensions 7
of Learning Designs

Technical, Psychological/
Emotional, and Social

"Leaders actively engage with policy makers and decision makers so that resources, policies, annual calendars, daily schedules, and structures support professional learning to increase student achievement."

—Standards for Professional Learning

"What makes activities conducive to flow is that they are designed to make optimal experience easier to achieve. They have rules which require the learning of skills, they set up goals, they provide feedback, and they make control possible."

—Mihaly Csikszentmihalyi

"To transform systems, incentives should be structured to promote collaboration and knowledge sharing, rather than competition, across organizations."

—Linda Darling-Hammond

In this chapter, the following questions are addressed:

- What are three dimensions of learning designs and why are they important?

Technical—how, where, when, and what do you learn?

Psychological/Emotional—is the learning meaningful and relevant for you?

Social—how can we learn together?

- Why should the three dimensions be considered when designing professional learning?
- How do the three dimensions of the Five-Part Plan (FPP) link job-embedded learning opportunities to the evaluation system?

At the end of this chapter, you will be able to

- identify the characteristics of three dimensions of learning designs—technical, psychological/emotional, and social; and
- describe how the FPP integrates the three dimensions of designing job-embedded professional learning linked to teacher evaluation.

THE CONTEXT OF TEACHER EVALUATION

In May, several principals, teacher leaders, and I engaged in conversations about the new teacher evaluation system to be implemented in the upcoming school year. As I listened to educators, similar concerns were voiced. First, how can teachers improve and grow in effectiveness as measured by the teacher evaluation rubric? Where will they find the time? Second, how can teacher evaluation be perceived as a "growth" not a "gotcha" place? Third, since teachers are now directed to be in their classrooms and not pulled out for professional development, how will they have opportunities for ongoing professional learning? Fourth, since teachers' time for collaboration in weekly professional learning communities (PLCs) is to be used exclusively for data analysis, grade-level management, and sharing information, where can they learn practices to support students' needs? Teachers in three of the four schools could no longer choose how they used their PLC time. As one teacher, Cathryn, states in her reflections,

> There is quite a bit of research on [PLCs] and even more *mis*-enactments of these communities in schools across the country. PLCs often turn into smaller versions of staff meetings where day-to-day business is discussed. While this is a necessary component of school structures, these meetings do not constitute professional learning communities.

Reflections like the one written by Cathryn and many conversations with principals and teacher leaders show that clearly the need exists for teachers to find time during the school day to learn how to be effective as measured through teacher evaluation, have choice in their learning, feel that they are supported, and have time to collaborate with others. As a response to principal concerns and teacher needs, the FPP was developed integrating three dimensions of professional learning—technical (time and place for learning), psychological/emotional (reason to learn, teacher choice in the learning), and social (in collaboration with others).

WHAT ARE THREE DIMENSIONS OF LEARNING DESIGNS, AND WHY ARE THEY IMPORTANT?

Three dimensions of professional learning—technical, psychological, and social—informed the creation and development of the FPP, which is used to structure the school year for job-embedded professional learning. In my thirty years as a professional educator, I have learned all three dimensions are critical for professional learning to be *meaningful* to teachers. It must have the important and useful qualities that engage teachers' minds and hearts. Professional learning is most meaningful when teachers have time and opportunity to gain knowledge and skills and see the relevance for engaging in the learning design. They must also have a voice in deciding the content and design for their learning; know that the learning design acknowledges teacher's experience, professionalism, and skills; and is collaborative. In this chapter, we will explore each dimension and identify how it integrates with the FPP.

Technical Dimension

The technical dimension refers to the techniques, procedures, and structures for professional learning. This dimension uses data for monitoring and assessing progress, and addresses several important questions. What, when, where, and how do I learn, and how well did I learn and apply the new knowledge? Richard Elmore (2004) informs us that to improve instruction, teachers must focus on learning in the *instructional core*, which is defined as the interaction of the students and teacher, students with each other, and with the content in the classroom. Focusing on the instructional core means that teachers must simultaneously work on improving their knowledge and skills, the student's level of engagement in learning, and the rigor of the content. The next section details how the FPP uses the technical dimension for professional learning.

What do teachers need to know how to do?

During Part 1 of the FPP, two teacher evaluation domains—Creating an Environment for Learning and Teaching for Learning—identify indicators for what all teachers should know and be able to do effectively in the classroom. Part 2 involves teachers choosing a learning design where they learn how to increase effectiveness for creating a collaborative learning environment, use instruction that increases student engagement, and use formative assessment for ongoing monitoring of student understanding. During Part 3A, teachers schedule time to actively engage in Cycle 1 of the three-part lesson-design cycle. After Part 3A, multiple data sources, such as short-cycle assessment, student work artifacts, student and teacher reflections, and teacher evaluation observations, are analyzed for more specific teacher and student needs. What do students need to improve? What do teachers need to learn to support the students? Results of this data inform the teachers' learning focus for Part 3B—implementation of learning design Cycle 2. The learning focus for Cycle 2 was informed from analysis of the data collected after Cycle 1.

Where? Part 1 and Part 2 occurred in a large space, like the library, for the three elementary schools. Parts 3A and 3B—Learning Design Cycles required a room for planning and reflection, and one teacher's classroom for implementation. Some teams planned online through Zoom or Google conferencing, then reflected during school hours. Parts 4 and 5 also occurred in the library or a teacher's classroom.

When? Two lesson design cycles were scheduled in August and dates put on the school's calendar. Teachers decided the exact dates within windows of time. Cycle 1 was implemented between late September and November, and Cycle 2 between January and February. The goal was to implement a minimum of two lesson design cycles before the state testing window, which began in March.

How? Part 3—learning designs cycles—were implemented in two ways:

1. Teams blocked off three hours of uninterrupted time, from 8:00 to 11:00, and 12:00 to 3:00, and substitute teachers hired for a full day rotated between classes. For example, if Vertical Team Study met in the morning, the substitute teachers supervised their classes, and then rotated to the Lesson Design group classes in the afternoon.

2. Teachers planned on one day, either after school or via online conferencing, and implemented the lesson together the following day, then reflected after school.

Some schools were limited in the amount of money they could spend on substitutes, so they implemented the cycle in chunks. The one nonnegotiable was that teams must share the lesson enactment and learning in the classroom together.

How well? Multiple data sources were used to inform each teacher's focus for learning in Cycle 3B. Student reflections, artifacts, short-cycle assessments, and principal observations were analyzed and used. In conversations with teachers, principals were able to communicate changes they saw in teacher practice. For example, one principal observed more student-to-student engagement, and that "students are talking more with each other and using appropriate content vocabulary," which was one of the focus areas in the Peer Teaching design. Another principal observed that "there are more higher level questions being asked during the lesson"—the focus for the Lesson Design team. Parts 4 and 5—Sharing Knowledge and Creating the Professional Knowledge Base—gave Learning Design teams an opportunity to share publicly what was learned, and identify knowledge to remember.

Educators say . . .

"What I found most valuable in the FPP was how organized everything felt. I know what I needed to do, but more importantly, I knew how to do it."

"The protocols were structured yet open for interpretation."

"The plan is simple and manageable, and gives me a concrete framework to provide sustainable professional learning throughout the year."

Psychological/Emotional Dimension

The psychological/emotional dimension is that aspect of teaching that promotes self-efficacy and relevancy in the learning experience. This dimension addresses the following questions:

- Is this session relevant and meaningful for me?
- Will I learn what I need to support my growth and my students' growth?
- Do I have input that influences decisions affecting my professional learning?

The psychological/emotional dimension refers to one's affect, enjoyment, and purpose, leading to the "making of meaning" (Csikszentmihalyi, 1990). Mihaly Csikszentmihalyi, from his extensive research of optimal experiences, reveals that what makes an experience genuinely satisfying is a state of consciousness called "flow." Flow describes an optimal experience that is positive, enjoyable, and meaningful for the participant. According to this research, four elements must be present for learning to have meaning and be enjoyable to the learners:

1. Clear goals

2. Required skills to reach the goals

3. Feedback on progress toward the goal

4. The ability to control the activity

Experiencing flow enhances enjoyment and the quality of teaching, learning, and life. Teachers who experience flow describe it as having uninterrupted time to learn, practice, and be creative, both individually and in collaboration with other teachers. They also have time to design and teach lessons; receive feedback from the principals, students, and other teachers; and control when and how the lesson is taught. Teachers face psychological and emotional challenges when external demands for improving their performance increases, while time for learning and practice with feedback decreases or disappears.

Lisa, an experienced, highly effective high school math teacher comments, "I can only be creative when I am not in survival mode." Flow does not happen for teachers when lessons are mandated and prescriptive, when there are frequent interruptions by visitors or intercom messages, when students are constantly tested, when external initiatives demand constant teacher attention, when data analysis consumes all the PLC time, or when teachers lack control to change the situation. Active engagement in two cycles of the same learning design produced a flow situation for the teachers—they established their own goals for learning, studied the knowledge and skills they needed, received feedback from students and other teachers, and controlled when and where they planned and engaged in the learning design.

Social cognitive theory suggests that teachers perform best when they have "human agency," and can exercise some influence over what they do (Bandura, 2006a). From social cognitive theory emerged the idea of *teacher self-efficacy*, or the acknowledgement that teacher's beliefs in their own ability to plan, organize, and carry out activities affect the quality of the outcomes of those activities (Bandura, 2006a; Skaalivick & Skaalvick, 2010). Efficacy beliefs determine how teachers perceive learning opportunities, effect their choice of learning activity, and impact how much effort is expended on an activity. When educators provide input into decisions about the content, context, and design of professional learning, it becomes meaningful to them. Successful outcomes then become more likely and can increase job satisfaction and reduce teacher turnover.

The following section includes an outline how the FPP uses the psychological/emotional dimension to enhance professional learning.

Part 1—Teachers' self-efficacy is activated when each teacher is *asked* to write five practices on sticky notes, one practice per note, that should be visible in every classroom every day. What do they believe supports students' learning?

The action of *asking teachers first* honors their professionalism, experiences, and skills. Next, the entire school staff correlates the five agreed-on practices to the teacher evaluation rubric so teachers come to know if what they believe is substantiated by research. Instead of *telling* teachers to study the teacher evaluation descriptors first, teachers are *asked* to match their professional knowledge with the rubric. At the four schools, each of the five practices chosen by staff aligned to between one and four domain elements.

Part 2—Teacher self-efficacy was again activated when teachers selected a learning design, resulting in teachers expending effort and energy actively engaging in two Learning Design Cycles to attain given learning goals.

Part 3—Learning Design Cycles were intentionally designed to promote the four elements of flow. During the planning phase, teachers created goals for themselves and for student outcomes, such as how to ask higher-level questions and how to promote increased student-to-student engagement. During planning, teachers studied, by reading articles and observing videos, then learned what skills were needed to reach the goals. During lesson enactment in the classroom, teachers implemented new learning and received feedback from students and team teachers. All four elements of flow can occur during the lesson design cycles—teachers set clear goals, identified the required skills to reach those goals, and controlled when they implemented the cycle and what lesson and skills to develop.

Parts 4 and 5—Teachers felt empowered to produce knowledge, rather than transmit knowledge through the Learning Design Cycles, then share with other teachers. Two teams who engaged in Video Study with Application practiced the formative assessment strategy described in the video "My Favorite No," from the Teaching Channel, and adapted the delivery to meet their students' needs. When teachers are knowledge producers, and not knowledge transmitters, it might sound like: "We are working on the same strategy as the teacher in the video"—rather than, "We are doing the same thing as the teacher in the video."

Educators say . . .

"I enjoyed getting grounded in common practices that we can agree as nonnegotiable characteristics of our math classes."

"I enjoyed having time to be able to practice new things in my class, as some practices require more time for teachers and students to get used to and learn to do them."

Social Dimension

The social dimension addresses how teachers work and learn together through collaboration. Effective teacher collaboration can be defined as engaging in regular routines where teachers talk about classroom experiences to strengthen knowledge and develop expertise in teaching and learning, and to support each other in trying new things (Davis, 2003; Rennie Center for Education Research and Policy, 2014). Research shows teachers highly value working with each other and using each other's strengths to innovate and improve practice (Edmondson, 2012). Furthermore, higher levels of teacher collaboration correlate with increased student performance (Goddard, Goddard, & Tschannen-Moran, 2007). Structures supporting teacher collaboration on school campuses typically include PLCs, learning teams, and learning designs, such as Lesson Design and Peer Teaching.

Imagine you are a teacher in the high-stakes context of accountability that measures your job performance based on both teaching effectiveness and student scores on state assessments. What if your job or increases in your salary are dependent on student test scores? And what if you no longer have any time to learn to improve your practice—either inside your school during work hours, or outside of school because there is no money for professional development? The time you once had to learn during the school day—during PLCs or regular weekly meetings—is now gone. You are given time by administrators to meet face-to-face in PLCs to analyze data, but learning what to do with that data is now on your own time. Consequently, many teachers now spend long hours at home searching online for ideas and support from professional organizations, such as Learning Forward. The FPP addresses this problem by purposefully designing the school year for teachers to have between six and twelve hours of time to collaborate in whole group, small group, or virtual learning settings.

In the next section, we provide a detailed look at how the FPP uses the social dimension to further support teacher learning.

Part 1—Teachers meet as whole group staff to create a shared vision of effective classroom learning environments by reaching consensus on five practices that should present daily in every classroom. The group then aligns these five practices with teacher evaluation descriptors.

Part 2—Teachers select learning designs, then form teams based on individual interest.

Part 3—Teachers share classroom enactment of practices with other teachers through active engagement in the classroom experience.

Part 4—Teacher teams share learning from implementation of design cycles in teams with whole school staff.

Part 5—Collective knowledge produced from engaging in learning cycles is collected, archived, and made accessible to everyone.

Educators say . . .

"I enjoyed collaborating and team teaching with a colleague, because it allowed me to see changes I could make in my own classroom."

"The [FPP] built continuity within the department."

"I particularly liked team teaching with the other Algebra II teacher. We got to observe each other's methods of instruction and the students enjoyed learning with two teachers."

"By participating in the [FPP], we were able to focus deeply on one or more practices. Which, in turn, allowed us to strengthen the practice we felt was the weakest."

WHY SHOULD ALL THREE DIMENSIONS BE CONSIDERED WHEN DESIGNING PROFESSIONAL LEARNING?

Reason 1—Allows teachers the time and structures to learn through a focus on teaching quality

Reason 2—Provides teachers optimal, meaningful learning experiences to learn skills, set up goals, provide feedback, and make control possible

Reason 3—Creates time for teachers to enjoy learning through collaboration

Grace, a high school math department chair in her fifth year of teaching at a high-achieving, high-poverty, rural high school maintains a positive attitude, willingness to learn, and high expectations for students. She participated in a two-year teacher leader program, where she built her mathematics content and pedagogical knowledge resulting in an increase in student achievement as measured by state tests and short-cycle assessments. Grace is far from a "slacker." She is well respected as a highly effective teacher who generates energy toward change and support for students—a veritable gem of a teacher to value, respect, and retain at a campus.

Grace recently described the challenges faced by the math department for finding time to learn professionally.

> We were hit with a million things—more busy stuff and disruptions than ever before and it's been very frustrating and hard to deal with. My team is just unhappy with many things we cannot control right now unrelated to the professional learning design. Like having instructional time taken away a lot. We had SBA retakes at the end of September. Teachers were pulled out to administer testing. We had short-cycle testing yet the regional evaluation system messed up really bad and delayed our testing for two weeks, so there were days we planned to test and didn't, so we didn't have lesson plans, then there were days we had to reschedule short-cycle testing and lost instructional time! We had homecoming week where classes were disrupted every day. We had End of Course [EOC] retakes where teachers were pulled out to administer testing, then teachers were pulled out to grade the EOCs, and now we are going through an accreditation process where teachers have been pulled out to collect evidence and each one of us has had to create a *huge* evidence binder to support Domains 1–4 [of teacher evaluation] and accreditation. So with that said, our [FPP] learning design project we had been excited about at the beginning of the year sort of became a *scramble* to get it done.

Grace's reflection highlights the to day-to-day challenges of school life faced by teachers who want to collaborate and focus on improving instruction, yet are caught up in uncontrollable situations that take precious time away from instruction. At the beginning of the school year, the teachers were enthusiastic about choosing a learning design and the opportunity to work together. As one teacher put it, "We are excited to . . . choose to study something together and try it in a classroom setting, reflect, and share learning with one another." Her statement reinforces the need to consider both the psychological and social dimensions of learning designs—the need for choice—a place of personal control in the midst of doing tasks teachers can't control, and the opportunity to collaborate during the learning. As Linda Darling-Hammond (2012) states in the opening quote, "To transform systems, incentives should be structured to promote collaboration and knowledge sharing" (p. 37). She adds that "knowledge-sharing is needed to develop not only learning organizations but a learning-oriented system of education in which ongoing evaluation and inquiry into practice are stimulated within and across classrooms."

One can imagine potential pitfalls for Grace and the team if only one of the dimensions of professional learning is used for professional learning.

By adhering to the technical dimension only, teachers may have time, structures, and resources for learning, and even multiple sources of data for monitoring and evaluating, but the activities may not be professionally meaningful, relevant, enjoyable, or connected to theirs or students' needs, or be enacted in collaboration with other teachers. If only the technical dimension is considered, district-level administrators, who require teachers to attend "trainings" away from their campus on professional development staff-release days, might choose inadequate professional learning without consulting the teachers. When guided only by the technical dimension, the content of the learning sessions may not be relevant or connected to teacher/student needs, as teachers sometimes complain when administrators or instructional coaches choose the agendas.

When we make choices guided by the psychological/emotional dimension only, it may feel good but lack substance. If principals support teachers choosing learning designs only because the activity is enjoyable, he/she may find their time investment is not connected to substantive learning. A possible outcome under this scenario happens when money is allocated for teachers to attend conferences of their choice without accountability. There may be no plan for application of learning into practice, or sharing of learning with other colleagues, or consideration of shared goals. Everyone is happy, but limited resources are wasted.

Finally, imagine what may happen when only the social dimension is valued. Teachers may have time to meet regularly in PLCs or learning teams, work with each other, and attend professional learning sessions and conferences, but there is no shared vision, goals, guidance, monitoring, or accountability. Collaborating and meeting with each other may enhance relationships, but without the balancing of all three dimensions, it is unlikely this tactic by itself will result in positive change in student learning.

My claim is that through a structured model, such as the FPP, schools can be purposefully designed so all three dimensions—the technical, psychological/emotional, and social—promote the emergence of a collaborative school culture of collective responsibility that focuses on continuous improvement in instruction for student learning. The following chart shows how each phase of the FPP utilizes this multidimensional approach.

HOW DO THE THREE DIMENSIONS OF THE FIVE-PART PLAN LINK JOB-EMBEDDED LEARNING OPPORTUNITIES TO THE EVALUATION SYSTEM?

Teacher evaluation does not have to be a bitter pill to swallow—it can be considered as a vitamin promoting growth for student learning *only if*

Table 7.1 Dimensions Aligned to FPP

	Technical	Psychological / Emotional	Social
Part 1—Reaching Consensus	• Identifies classroom practices aligned with teacher evaluation elements	• Honors teachers professionalism, experience, and skills	• Creates shared vision together
Part 2—Selecting Designs	• Selects design based on data	• Selects design based on interest and need	• Selects design collaboratively
Part 3—Implementing Learning Design Cycles	• Plans a lesson with intentionally focus aligned to Five Agreements • Implements the lesson • Reflects/assesses using student artifacts	• Chooses lesson to plan • Decides goals • Identifies skills to meet the goals • Receives feedback on progress toward the goal, and controls the activity	• Plans a lesson collaboratively • Shares lesson enactment with others • Reflects with others
Part 4—Sharing Knowledge	• Shares knowledge individually	• Produces knowledge	• Shares learning with whole school staff
Part 5—Creating a Professional Knowledge Base	• Documents knowledge based on results measured by data	• Chooses knowledge to document	• Documents knowledge collectively and shared by others

supportive conditions exist for teachers to learn. The FPP is an example of a support system that creates a technically rich, psychologically safe, non-evaluative structure for teachers to focus on learning collaboratively. Professional learning opportunities must align with teacher evaluation to support the improvement of teachers. Schools must link both formal professional development and job-embedded learning opportunities to the evaluation system (Darling-Hammond, 2012). The FPP not only linked the teachers job-embedded learning experiences to teacher evaluation through active engagement in the two cycles of learning designs (technical dimension), but also created an enjoyable "flow" experience for teachers, enhanced teacher self-efficacy (psychological dimension), and promoted collaboration toward shared goals (social dimension).

YOUR TURN—START THE CONVERSATION

1. What dimensions are considered when designing professional learning experiences for teachers at your school?

2. How are the three dimensions addressed for teacher professional learning at your school?

3. How do teachers see the teacher evaluation system at your school—as a "growth" opportunity or a "gotcha"?

4. If your school has a PLC, how is the time used? How much time do teachers spend analyzing data versus learning how to do something differently with the data findings?

Building a School's $\mathbf{8}$ Professional Knowledge Base

"Collective work in trusting environments provides a basis for inquiry and reflection into teachers' practice, allowing teachers to take risks, solve problems, and attend to dilemmas in their practice."

—Linda Darling-Hammond

"The fact that everyday millions of teachers produce knowledge of teaching, it is worth examining what would be needed to transform teachers' knowledge into a professional knowledge base for teaching."

—James Hiebert, Ronald Gallimore, and James Stigler (2002)

"We learned and don't want to forget how to engage students in peer feedback. When students looked at each others' work and started to ask each other questions, the questions helped them analyze each other's strategies and ways of thinking."

—Dave, high school mathematics teacher

In this chapter, the following questions are addressed:

- What is a Professional Knowledge Base (PKB)?
- Why should a school consider building a PKB?

- What PKBs were created after implementing the Five-Part Plan (FPP)?
- What worked, didn't work, and what can be done differently to create a PKB?

At the end of this chapter, you will be able to

- define a PKB;
- name reasons a school should consider building and maintaining a PKB;
- identify the professional knowledge teachers at three schools want to remember; and
- identify successes and challenges with creating a PKB, and suggestions for improvement.

THE DATA MEETING

During a fourth-grade team meeting in late October, four teachers and one instructional coach analyzed results from short-cycle assessment data.

Teacher 1	We went up in the geometry domain!
Teacher 2	Yes, our students always score well on geometry items.
Teacher 3	Look at the fraction questions. They are so low.
Instructional Coach	I noticed that the most of the test items that students scored low in are multi-step problems.
Teacher 1	Yes, multi-step problems are so hard for our kids. Our textbook doesn't give students enough practice with them.
Instructional Coach	We need to think about how students can improve on fraction problems and have more time to practice problem solving using multi-step.
Teacher 2	We just need to give students more time on what they need to practice.

Exchanges similar to the conversation above occur much too frequently among school-based educators after receiving data. Hoorays and smiles abound if scores increase, as do moans and grimaces when they go down. The teachers and coach in the above conversation explained what increased and decreased. Absent from this conversation were *questions to explore*—to probe for root causes as to why the problem exists and generate strategies for changing the situation. For example, why do fourth-grade students typically score higher on geometry items? Is the way geometry is taught and learned contributing to student success? Why are students scoring lower on fraction problems? What misconceptions do students have? How do we know what to do differently? What actions can we take?

WHAT IS A PROFESSIONAL KNOWLEDGE BASE?

Just imagine if school-based educators had a school's history of learning archived in a database that was easily retrievable. They could login to the school's PKB, where they might find the "fraction file" that identifies why previous classes of fourth graders have struggled with fraction problems, and find tested lessons and strategies that resulted in better student understanding. Perhaps the teachers and coach could draw on a repository of knowledge that resulted in an improved outcome for students in a previous school year. What if the coach or designated teacher leader takes the responsibility to archive the knowledge so it was readily accessible to all teachers at the school? According to Hiebert, Gallimore, and Stigler (2002), a PKB is body of knowledge created by practitioners in the classroom that can be readily accessed and shared broadly with other professionals. Their claim is that "to improve classroom teaching in a steady, lasting way, the profession needs a knowledge base that grows and improves" (p. 1). Time for PLCs is too short already without having to solve the same teaching problems year after year!

Let's think about knowledge—facts, information, and skills acquired by a person through experiences or education—and how knowledge can either be transmitted or constructed. The distinction between these similar terms is that knowledge *transmission* implies the passive assimilation of given knowledge, where as knowledge *construction* occurs when teachers start to see their work as an active, essential effort to advance the field of education (Scardamalia & Bereiter, 2006). As knowledge constructors, when a problem of practice arises, teachers could study, try solutions together, learn what supports and doesn't support their students' advancement, then document the learning to remember. As knowledge transmitters, outside "experts" guide teachers to solutions to be passed on through them. Perhaps if teachers saw themselves as pro-active knowledge constructors rather than passive knowledge transmitters, an untapped potential might be unleashed. For example, after studying formative assessment strategies from research and articles, teachers as knowledge constructors might claim, "we are working on the same problem as Dylan Wiliam" (referring to the expert on formative assessment). The knowledge transmitter might only offer, "We should read Dylan Wiliam to find out what to do."

When teachers perceive themselves as producers of practice knowledge, this supports teacher self-efficacy and can be professionally empowering, rather than feeling that answers always come from the experts. The results could be a database with readily accessible files that contain lessons, strategies, activities, and interventions that have been tried in *their* classrooms and that work for *their* students at *their* school.

From my years of various and broad experiences facilitating professional learning with educators (teachers, instructional coaches, principals, district administrators, superintendents) at all levels of school systems, and hundreds of hours learning alongside educators in their schools, teachers typically draw on and value knowledge published by others—not each other or their own evidenced-based experiences—to inform and improve their practice. It is the rare teacher, indeed, who claims to have constructed his/her own practitioner knowledge drawn from classroom experiences. It begs the question: Can teachers value each other's knowing and learning from practice or must they always look outward to experts to seek answers and solutions to problems of practice? Are the solutions to their students' needs within their own system guided by research and experience? When a problem arises, such as how we can have an effective professional learning community (PLC), or how we can increase student to student engagement, teachers often look to websites, articles, videos, books, and magazines for activities and ideas. What would happen if teachers had opportunities, support, and encouragement to construct their own knowing with other teachers in their building? The result could be a knowledge based on instructional strategies tried in their classroom that produces successful student results. Student voices could be included, as well.

Consider the following two examples:

Drawing from Constructed Knowledge—Over the years, Sienna, a teacher at Hamos Elementary, learned to create a positive learning environment where most students questioned each other in small groups and engaged in lively classroom discussions. During implementation of the Vertical Team Study design, her fellow teachers at Hamos noticed that the students in Sienna's class interacted differently than in their classrooms. What was happening, and what actions did the teachers take that resulted in student-to-student engagement using questioning? Sienna claimed that student-to-student questioning starts on the first day of school with teacher modeling. "I act as if I am the student and model the way to be curious with each other respectfully." Sienna described the steps used during the first month of school that resulted in the classroom "questioning" dynamic. Sienna constructed practice knowledge for how to promote classroom discourse—an element measured on the teacher evaluation rubric. Perhaps if

Sienna documented this process (and others like it), then filed it in the school's PKB, other teachers, instructional coaches, and principals would soon have an accessible repository of "how-to" strategies to promote effective teaching, which could also be aligned to a school's evaluation system.

Drawing from the Knowledge of Others—A third-grade team ends the year with over 60% of the students scoring below or near proficient on state test scores. Although disappointed in the test results, the teachers are optimistic and hopeful for a clean slate in the upcoming school year— a new start—to do things differently for improved results.

The teachers attend a summer institute where they learn to increase student engagement using questioning techniques by studying articles, watching videos, and observing teachers who model these strategies with students in a lab setting. At the end of the day, one teacher asks, How do we do this? "I just wish Jenna [the teacher facilitating learning in the lab setting with students] could come to my classroom and start the year for me." The teacher does not say, " I will practice and develop the same strategies I see Jenna using with students," implying that she wants someone else to transmit the knowledge for her.

Part 5 of the FPP asks school-based educators to create a PKB for their school—to document what they have learned, build on successes, and abandon practices that didn't prove effective in student achievement.

WHY SHOULD A SCHOOL CONSIDER BUILDING A PROFESSIONAL KNOWLEDGE BASE?

A school should consider building a PKB to ensure continuity of excellence and growth over time, despite teacher and principal turnover. Improving teaching is currently situated in a "graying and greening" trend, as the age distribution of teachers has a large proportion of teachers either in their first year or past age 50 (Ingersoll & Merrill, 2010). Principal turnover is also a contributing factor to teaching quality leading to student results. Research indicates that high principal turnover leads to greater teacher turnover (Béteille, Kalogrides, & Loeb, 2011; Fuller, Baker, & Young, 2007) and can lead to teachers not investing in changes for student improvement (Hargreaves, 2003).

What happens when a school experiences high teacher and principal turnover? It is like starting every year anew—with no history of learning at that school and no record of strategies that worked or didn't work to support student achievement.

What impacts student learning more than any factor? A high-quality effective teacher who uses research-based strategies to create a learning environment for all students to succeed.

What would the legal, business, or medical professions be like if they did not have a knowledge base that aggregates with time? When we apply parallel scenarios from the legal, business, and medical professional to the current trends in schools, it highlights the absurdity of this situation.

Legal Profession—Every time a case is tried in court, there are no prior cases to draw from.

Medical Profession—Every time you need a knee replacement, the doctor has to invent a new procedure.

Business—Every time there is a new business start-up, there is no economic data to draw from and it is unknown whether it is a good business environment.

With a repository of knowledge in place, schools can keep advancing successes. Without a repository, the same mistakes keep reoccurring. As the education profession is "graying" with experienced teachers leaving, and "greening" with new teachers starting, then perhaps our schools can only maintain a consistent high quality if new teachers have access to a school's PKB. Every year, teachers learn what works and doesn't work to support student achievement, yet if this learning is archived, the knowledge needed for the successes can accrue and build over time.

WHAT PROFESSIONAL KNOWLEDGE BASES WERE CREATED AFTER IMPLEMENTING THE FIVE-PART PLAN?

Three of the four schools that implemented the FPP—Chavez, Hamos, and Terra—engaged in Part 5—Creating a Professional Knowledge Base. What knowledge did learning design teams want to remember and archive? During Part 4—Sharing Professional Knowledge with Whole School Staff—teams shared their experiences and learning, both verbally and in writing, from their active participation in Part 3, two cycles of their chosen learning design.

At Chavez High School, Grace, the math department chair, states,

We have a professional knowledge base at our school through the math department evidence binder. The five agreements were placed in the binder along with the reflections from the Knowledge Showcase. The biggest gain we had out of our five agreements was an increase in formative assessment and displaying student work.

Table 8.1 Three Schools Professional Knowledge Base

School	Five Agreements	Add to Knowledge Base
Chavez High School	• Summarize everyday • Use interactive notebooks • Use high-level questioning • Student work has meaningful feedback • Use word wall with visual representation Other • Using formative assessment	• Ask students to summarize, instead of the teacher summarizing—preselect the strategies prior to students sharing • No information shared • Use "Levels of Cognitive Demand" chart to guide questions toward a higher level, and encourage student-to-student questioning • Engage students in peer feedback process • Use anchor charts and compendiums • Use "My Favorite No" from the Teaching Channel for formative assessment and building a culture for critiquing the reasoning of others (Common Core Math Practice 3)
Hamos Elementary	• Teachers and students engage in learning and assessment • Positive learning environment • Students question, defend their thinking, and talk, talk, talk about content • Lesson goals and objectives are clear • Small groups/differentiated instruction	• Use video design websites to learn to design engaging activities with technology • Use exit cards, and plus/deltas on a daily basis • Model the voice tone, behaviors, and phrases that students should use • Focus students on a shared goal, as in the One World Soccer Ball Project • Model the language and behavior you want students to exhibit the first month of school • Model student to student questioning as if you were a student • Use daily learning targets and criteria for success • Ask students to keep a journal and write what they learned • Design activities using technology, such as Leap Pad, and SMART Board for small group activities and as a response to intervention

(Continued)

Table 8.1 (Continued)

School	Five Agreements	Add to Knowledge Base
Terra Elementary	• High levels of student engagement • Language rich environment, content vocabulary • Evidence of understanding using questioning and student modeling • Collaborative, cooperative learning environment where students are respectful and have ownership of their learning • Encourage problem solving and critical thinking skills	• High leverage practices is a tool for choosing research practices that result in active student engagement • Number sense routines • Identified how to use three talk moves—Turn and Talk, Revoicing, Tell Me More • Use the activity from the "Making Ten with Popsicle Sticks" (Teaching Channel) to assess K–1 students math fluency • Identified four strategies that increased respectful climate for learning • Third-grade lesson developed on the distributive property from Lesson Design • Developed activities that support students making conjectures • Collaborative planning uncovers our different interpretations of the standards • Process developed to transcribe short cycle test items into Spanish using a technology program

WHAT WORKED, WHAT DIDN'T WORK, AND WHAT CAN BE DONE DIFFERENTLY TO CREATE A PROFESSIONAL KNOWLEDGE BASE?

Awareness of the concept of a PKB for a school campus was generated. Chavez teachers provided us with the most concrete PKB—their "evidence binder"—that provided the math teachers accessible solutions to recurring problems of practice. The experience of creating a PKB plants the seed that teachers are capable of producing knowledge linked to practice, and that their learning—mistakes and all—are worthy of being shared. Because of this method of sharing learning, teachers have access to concrete, detailed, and specific solutions for their own problems of practice. Teacher to teacher communication is a language of how to do, not what to do, which results in active staff engagement during the Knowledge Showcase. The possibilities of a viable, usable, and accessible PKB was planted at each school so that educators could learn from the past and not repeat mistakes. As Maya Angelou said, "Those who know better, do better."

What did not work was the lack of formalization of the PKB at two of the three schools. After Part 4—Sharing Professional Knowledge with Whole School Staff—no decisions were made as to the location for storing information, or identifying a categorizing system for access and retrieval. A follow-up plan did not exist at the elementary schools at the end of the year; consequently, no one took the initiative to finalize the PKB. It just wasn't on anyone's radar. Cathryn, a teacher at Terra Elementary, states,

> I hope we can do better in Part 5 next year because I can see how this is important to make our learning concrete. I think we need to do our sharing a bit earlier so we're not all too tired to develop a Professional Knowledge Base.

Just before the Knowledge Showcase, Krista, the principal at Terra Elementary, found out that she would be transferred to a turnaround school, and Maria, principal at Hamos Elementary, retired. Gainfield never held the Knowledge Showcase due to demands placed on them by the turnaround school project. The staff's work pace accelerated when each school underwent multiple changes and created tasks that competed for time. Hence, the manifestation of a PKB envisioned by Hiebert et al. (2002) remains elusive. However, there is reason to be hopeful. Teachers, principals, and coaches actively participated and valued many things about creating a PKB. I believe that given time, Part 5—Creating a Professional Knowledge Base—can be an important tool for quality teaching.

YOUR TURN—START THE CONVERSATION

1. Do you have a PKB at your campus? If yes, what does it look like? If no, what are your thoughts about starting one?

2. What would the benefits and challenges be to creating a schoolwide PKB?

3. How do teachers know what to do each year to improve their practice, resulting in increased student achievement?

Meaningful Learning to Remember

9

"Next year at the beginning of the school year, I plan on starting by pulling out the evidence binder and revisiting our Five Agreements and offer an opportunity to revise them. From here, we will create a plan to ensure our Five Agreements are evident in our classrooms. The learning we participated in with you helped build a foundation for creating our Five Agreements, which we strongly value."

—Grace, high school math department chair

"Next year, as we implement vertical professional learning designs, when you plan, implement, and reflect, we need to think more about the 'how' and not so much focus on the 'what.' In my mind the 'how' would be the strategy/new ideas versus the 'what' being the activity/ assignment. If we focus on the 'how,' the process can apply to more than one lesson or content area versus an activity that you will only do once. The 'how' can impact learning on a much larger scale, and the 'what' only impacts that one assignment."

—Krista, elementary principal

"We learned about vertical communication, how to be specific with planning to consider what was beneficial to support our students, how to connect the Five Agreements to our teaching for learning, and we figured out what we needed to change. And, we were excited to do this!"

—Second-grade elementary teacher

I n this chapter, the following questions are addressed:

- What was learned from implementing the Five-Part Plan (FPP)?
- Where does learning grow and transform from here?

At the end of this chapter, you will be able to

- identify new insights that emerged from implementing the FPP, and
- reflect with the author on next steps for transforming professional learning at a school site.

WHAT WAS LEARNED FROM IMPLEMENTING THE FIVE-PART PLAN IN ONE YEAR?

The FPP was created standing on the shoulders of giants. These "giants" include the people and organizations named throughout in this book, who contributed invaluable knowledge and research about professional learning, professional learning communities (PLCs), learning designs, leadership, adult learning theories, school improvement, "flow," teacher self-efficacy, and collaborative learning. The FPP structure is an attempt to put theory into practice in response to an authentic need. Clearly, there is a need for teachers to have time, place, and ownership to advance their learning to better support students. As a response to this need, the FPP is a thorough guide for schools to turn "what to do" into "how to do it." Now that some schools have used it for a full school year, it is time to assess whether the FPP is worth investing continued time, effort, and resources. If it is worth continuing, we must try to understand how it can be better. As a lens to look back at the first year of the FPP, we will use the three dimensions for professional learning—technical, psychological, and social—to interpret themes that surfaced from analysis of three data sources: written reflections, interviews, and site visit notes (see Chapter 7). We also consult educators who actively participated in the project. In this chapter, we look at the FPPs pros and cons, and some unexpected outcomes through the lens of each dimension.

The Technical Dimension

In Chapter 7, the technical dimension was described as the "nuts and bolts" of professional learning. This dimension includes the techniques, procedures, and structures for professional learning, and uses data to monitor progress. This technical aspect addresses the questions—what, when, where, and how do I learn, and how well did I learn and apply the new knowledge?

Benefits that emerged from the data include

- the simplicity and clarity of the plan,
- time for focused engagement in two Learning Design Cycles,
- the use of Five Agreements as focal points,
- explicit link to teacher evaluation, and
- authentic learning in the classroom.

Three "aha" moments include (1) the crucial role of the principal, who must see the big picture for the FPP and provide the necessary supportive conditions for implementation; (2) the role of a designated teacher leader/instructional coach as "linchpin" for implementing the FPP; and (3) seeing gradual changes in the classroom after active engagement in two cycles of learning designs.

Simple, Clear Plan—Principals and teachers liked the simplicity of the FPP and clarity of direction. All five parts had structure, clear guidance, and direction, yet allowed for flexibility to meet contextual needs, such as scheduling lesson design cycles. The timeline for implementation was mentioned as a way to identify future events so as not to double-book events, or schedule at the same time as other events. For example, being apprised of the Knowledge Showcase date made it easy to plan and prepare products. Dave, a high school teacher, commented, "This plan is just so clear. I know what do and what is expected for the entire year." A principal said, "This is exactly what I needed. This plan is so doable and manageable for supporting the teachers' learning."

Time for Focused Learning

Teachers gained access to a variety of job-embedded learning designs that were not available to them before implementation of the FPP. Prior to implementing the FPP in each school, the PLC was the only design offered as a place for gaining knowledge and skills, yet in three of the four schools, the PLC was not used as a learning place. Since PLC time was being used for data analysis and management tasks, the FPP answered a critical need to structure time for teachers to learn how better to support student learning.

Five Agreements as Focal Points

Having a shared vision is the hallmark of an effective school. A shared vision gets everyone on the same page, speaking the same language, and moving in the same direction toward shared goals. The Five Agreements developed in Part 1 of the FPP was mentioned in feedback by several teachers and two principals as a clear way to provide a shared vision for the staff, and shared focus for growth.

Authentic Learning in the Classroom

Teachers' and instructional coaches' learning was meaningful, relevant, and genuine because Learning Design Cycles connected shared learning experiences to the classroom. Teachers commented on how valuable it was to learn about their students alongside them during lessons. They appreciated not having to travel and leave sub-plans to go to regional professional development and hear about other teachers' students. Learning was with their students!

Link to Teacher Evaluation

The Five Agreements (those behaviors and practices that should be in every classroom every day) were identified by the whole school staff by drawing on their experiences and beliefs. After reaching consensus on the Five Agreements, teachers aligned them with teacher evaluation elements from Domains 2 and 3—Learning Environment and Teaching and Learning—which principals use to observe and rate teaching in the classroom.

Engaging in two cycles of lesson designs provided teachers a place to study, practice, and align learning to the Five Agreements. If teachers actively engaged in all five parts of the FPP, they were rated either "effective" or "highly effective" on teacher evaluation Domain 4—Professionalism. The four principals participating in the FPP all agreed that this links to evaluation was clear. The links are as follows:

- The FPP links to Domains 1 through 4 of the teacher evaluation system.
- Five Agreements link to Domains 2 and 3.
- Learning designs are the structure where teachers learn how to become more effective with the Five Agreements.
- During the "Planning" phase of the lesson design cycle, teachers plan using elements of Domain 1—Planning and Preparation.
- During the "Enact in the Classroom" phase of the lesson design cycle, teachers' actions align with Domains 2 and 3.
- Participating in all five parts of the FPP aligns with an effective rating on Domain 4.

Pivotal "Aha" Moments

Principal Must "Get it"

Implementing the FPP required a principal to understand the "bigger picture" for professional learning. Principals who realized its value quickly saw the link to teacher evaluation and the growth opportunities afforded teachers through participation in lesson design cycles. Hardly surprising was the level of importance of the principal role for whether or not the FPP could be implemented. If the principals' mind-set was to empower teachers in their learning and create a culture of continuous improvement, then the FPP appealed to them immediately. "This is *just* what I needed!" was Krista's and Maria's comment when they first heard about the FPP. At schools where the FPP was implemented with fidelity, principals saw the FPP as a vehicle for their vision and agenda, not as "something extra."

Teacher Leader/Instructional Coach as "Linchpins"

The designation of a teacher leader/instructional coach proved to be vital to sustaining implementation of the FPP. Each school had an informal, yet visible teacher leader/coach linchpin(s) that supported implementation at the site. They were the go-to persons when questions were asked, ensured Learning Design Cycles were scheduled and well facilitated, and communicated with the principal about issues that needed attention. When momentum waned during high stress times of the year, the teacher leaders/coaches kept the energy positive and upbeat through encouraging words.

Seeing Changes

Principals, teachers, and instructional coaches saw changes in student responses and engagement as a result of teachers' learning from two cycles of their selected learning designs. Change takes time, yet during the Knowledge Showcase, teachers described changes they made to their practice, as well as changes they observed in students. I didn't anticipate that the changes would be so recognizable in such a short time.

The Two Cons

The downside and challenges of the FPP included not enough time to design a lesson, the need for substitutes, and struggles to create a Professional Knowledge Base (PKB). One teacher remarked that she kept thinking about the lesson after one hour. Other teachers commented that one hour was realistic, as that is about the amount of time they spend per week planning lessons. Some teachers did not choose to schedule substitutes for a three-hour block of time, as they did not want to leave substitute plans. Finally, waiting until the end of the year to create a PKB was unrealistic. The amount of tasks to complete at the end of the year was overwhelming and time consuming. One solution is to start creating the PKB at the beginning of the year and add learning to it after Cycles 1 and 2 of the learning designs.

The Psychological/Emotional Dimension

The psychological/emotional dimension refers to the ability to find meaning and purpose in the learning experience, and for teachers to experience self-efficacy so teachers have influence over what and how they learn. The psychological dimension addresses the following questions:

- Is this session relevant and meaningful for me?
- Will I learn what I need to support my own and students' growth, or is this yet another session I have to go to that wastes my time?
- Do I have input that influences decisions affecting my professional learning?

Four themes surfacing from the data point to the importance of (1) teachers' choice in selection of learning designs, (2) designs that provide a place to nurture innovation and creative "juices," (3) learning opportunities that are nonevaluative, and (4) flexibility. One unexpected outcome was that many teachers said they enjoyed the process and had fun. In the midst of the overwhelming initiatives coming at the teachers at an accelerated pace, it was heartwarming to hear that over half of the teachers had fun at some point in the process.

Selecting Learning Designs Matter

Teachers highly valued the opportunity to select their own learning design, and to have a voice in shaping the content of their professional learning. When the Terra Leadership Team met to plan for implementation of the FPP for the upcoming year, they decided that every professional learning design team would have mixed grade levels. Each teacher selected his/her own learning design, and every team had a vertical configuration.

Place to Nurture Innovation and Creative Juices

The FPP afforded teachers the opportunity to explore their passions, take creative action, and try something new. Prior to the FPP, most teachers lacked the opportunity to try formative assessment strategies in their classrooms, create a respectful learning climate through students' poetry and written expression, engage in Lesson Design to better understand the distributive property in various math domains, or engage students in an international soccer ball program integrating state standards with cultural awareness. Teachers' comments indicated that they valued a creative space for learning.

Nonevaluative Nature of the Learning Designs

Teachers appreciated the nonevaluative nature of the learning designs. The designs created a "safe" structure for collaborative learning and provided teachers the opportunity to practice and deepen learning about the

Five Agreements without judgment. Teachers weren't told that they had to learn something specific to address deficits measured in formal principal observations. Teachers were enabled to choose their own learning designs and develop skills that could be calibrated and adjusted by feedback from student outcomes, and, in so doing, were also better prepared for formal evaluations. This process felt safe and supportive to them, and was solidly linked to their own students' struggles.

Flexibility

Educators commented that the FPP afforded both a high degree of structure and organization, as well as flexibility. Teachers could select learning designs, content, and focus for learning, and schedule design cycles within a time frame, but did not confine their learning to a specific date.

Surprise "Aha" Moment

Learning was fun and exciting. Teachers enjoyed collaborating with each other in the classroom and with others they normally do not encounter. Perhaps this could be a factor in reducing the problematic turnover the profession has seen in recent years.

The Social Dimension

The social dimension refers to how teachers work and learn together through collaboration. This means teachers engage in regular routines, allowing them the opportunity to communicate about classroom experiences in an effort to develop expertise in teaching and learning. In addition, collaboration provides support so teachers can try new things.

Two frequent themes from the data include (1) collaboration is a must and is highly valued, and (2) the Five Agreements provide a schoolwide, collective focus, a "team spirit," as well as a shared language. One surprise "aha" moment was how much teachers valued learning vertically.

Collaboration Is a Must

Collaboration was the most frequently mentioned and valued aspect of the FPP. Teachers valued time for learning in collaboration through the design cycles, and for sharing the learning in the classroom together. They felt supported by other teachers in ways they had never experienced. Teachers also valued collaborating vertically across grade levels and with other content areas.

Schoolwide Focus and Vision

The Five Agreements gave educators a schoolwide focus on facilitating learning, including a shared language and images of learning in classrooms. Because the Five Agreements were aligned with several teacher evaluation elements, principals aligned their feedback from classroom observations to teachers' focused learning in the Learning Design Cycles.

Surprise "Aha" Moments

Learning Vertically

Teachers frequently mentioned the importance of collaborating with teachers across grade levels to support students as they progress through the grade levels, which was lacking prior to implementation of the FPP.

Lack of Perceived Collaboration in Current Team Structures

Collaboration was mentioned frequently as a benefit of the FPP. Why? Teachers in years past met weekly, but it often did not feel like collaboration. At Chavez High School, the math department already interacted in a PLC, but what they really valued was collaboration in the classroom through peer teaching. At Hamos and Terra, teachers met in teams to analyze data and manage and disseminate information,. However, when teachers actively engaged in the cycles of learning designs that they chose, they experienced collaboration as *their* act of working together to produce or create something. One fifth-grade team stated during a whole group reflection,

> We worked as a team during the PLD [lesson design]. Working collaboratively, we got to see that we were all approaching the same lesson differently. We created a trust to observe and come up with constructive criticism when we talked about the different ways we taught the lessons.

One team member added, "The PLD experience taught me how to safely communicate with my group to improve a lesson. We improved our communication and created a strong lesson based on our five different interpretations of how it could be taught."

WHERE DOES LEARNING GROW AND TRANSFORM FROM HERE?

Transformation is a journey requiring a clear map to guide people when the winds of change blow through, sometimes at hurricane speed. Thoughtful principals at four schools were willing to implement the FPP to advance professional learning at their schools, and in doing so, were often rewarded with fresh insights from teachers experiencing learning collaboratively in real classroom settings. Teachers took ownership of their professional learning through voice and choice in the selection of learning designs, used and collected data, learned in community, addressed real issues of practice, and observed changes and improvement. The FPP structures provided time for teachers and instructional coaches to produce new knowledge and skills by setting goals, planning, and implementing lessons collaboratively in the classroom. The FPP enhanced teachers' professional learning experience through meaningful collaboration that promoted their growth aligned to teacher evaluation. As one teacher remarked, "Everybody got involved. Special teachers got involved. Where else have you seen teachers across the school working and learning together?"

What emerged?

What emerged included increased collaboration, changes in facilitating learning, and interactions among school-based educators that led to creative action. Teachers gained a greater degree of professional freedom and shared the responsibility to make changes for student improvements and achieve increased student outcomes. The FPP provided a coherent system that linked meaningful professional learning to student outcomes and the teacher evaluation process, and created "team spirit"—feelings of camaraderie and community among all school staff, enabling them to develop shared mutual goals, collaborate, and learn well together. It is too early for any data, but there is also hope that this might help lower teacher turnover by increasing job satisfaction.

What happens now?

Chavez High School—Chavez is the only school of the four that will experience stability in leadership and teachers: 78% of the teachers want to participate in the FPP next year. The primary reason cited by teachers for not wanting to participate is that the Learning Design Cycles take time. One teacher commented that designing lessons with a specific focus took twice as long as she thought. "I just kept thinking about the lesson," she said. Grace, the department chair, said the team will use the "evidence binder" (Knowledge Base) at the beginning of the school year to

> revisit the Five Agreements and offer teachers an opportunity to revise them. I also want to make a poster [of the Five Agreements] for all our teachers to have in their rooms. From here, we will create a plan to ensure our five agreements are evident in our classrooms.

The learning we participated in with you helped build a foundation for creating our five agreements, which we strongly value. Thanks for all your support you have offered :)

Hamos Elementary—Despite indications from teachers and instructional coach that they want to continue implementing the FPP next year, an imminent change in leadership has placed the program in limbo. Principal Maria retired, and the school, now designated a "turnaround school," will have a new principal. The staff awaits the direction of the new principal.

Gainfield Elementary—Even though staff began implementation of the FPP with excitement through engaging in Parts 1 through 3 throughout the year, Parts 4 and 5 were not completed. When Gainfield was told it would be a turnaround school, the staff began frequent planning meetings after school. Planning for the Knowledge Showcase just got to be "too much" for everyone to continue.

Terra Elementary—Similar to Hamos and Gainfield, Principal Krista was reassigned to a turnaround school, and Terra is getting a new principal. Before leaving, Krista and the leadership met to formalize a plan to continue professional learning designs (PLDs—Terra's term for the FPP). During the leadership team meeting, the team reviewed the Five Agreements: student engagement, collaborative/cooperative conversational grouping, organized environment with clear expectations for rules and procedures, language-rich environment (content vocabulary), and evidence of student understanding.

Cathryn and Bernadette state:

For our PLDs the leadership team decided:

1. We need to have more learning about explicit structures that support student collaboration and conversation during math. We talked about the couple of resources we have—many folks were interested in using those resources next year as part of their PLD.

2. We want to focus on feedback as a tool for assessing students' level of understanding. Four of us are going to facilitate a learning session on feedback at the beginning of the year. We have a renewed emphasis on communicating to students and parents about their learning. We'd also like to incorporate student-to-student feedback, hopefully.

3. Krista asked the question of the leadership team—what does our schoolwide engagement look like and how can we improve it? To me, I think this is a challenging question because students can be engaged for very different reasons. So, I'm not sure how far we got with this one in our building a knowledge base.

And so the learning grows . . .

Closing Reflections

It can be transformational when thoughtful educators connect and learn together despite challenges and strong external forces beyond their control. This past year was a year rich with powerful learning in partnership for four principals, three instructional coaches, five teacher leaders, sixty-two teachers, and myself—the university partner. We experienced professional learning at its finest—informed by data, collaborative, authentic, job-embedded, meaningful, and transformational. A structured plan was used along with a variety of learning designs, which included teacher voice and choice in selecting the designs. Implementing the FPP was challenging, rewarding, meaningful, and fun. Together, we were able to put theory into action and devise a detailed plan for teachers to grow in alignment with teacher evaluation, and in support of student learning. We produced knowledge on our own where it was needed and used others' knowledge and wisdom as guides for developing our process for professional learning. The four schools found they did not need expensive consulting organizations to provide professional learning for teachers away from their classrooms. What was needed was both *time* and a *plan* to build capacity internally, by learning both inside and outside teachers' classrooms using a variety of learning designs, active engagement, the power to develop and guide themselves, supportive leadership, peer support with feedback to learn and see changes, and data to assess progress. The FPP for designing schools for meaningful learning is not *the* answer, but it is *one* solution that responds to the need for teachers to learn, grow, change, and enjoy the process.

You are invited to join the dialogue by creating professional learning models and plans for your school then sharing your knowledge with the broader field. Who knows—your efforts could result in important contributions of knowledge and tools for creating schools as places that promote meaningful professional learning.

Just for now, we close the conversation space.

References

Bandura, A. (2006a). Guide for constructing self-efficacy scales. In F. Pajares & T. Urdan (Eds.), *Self-efficacy beliefs of adolescents* (pp. 307–337). Greenwich, CT: Information Age.

Bandura, A. (2006b). Toward a psychology of human agency. *Perspectives on Psychological Science, 1,* 164–180.

Benjamin, B. E., Yeager, A., & Simon, A. (2012). *Conversation transformation.* New York: McGraw-Hill.

Béteille, T., Kalogrides, D., & Loeb. S. (2011, July). *Stepping stones: Career paths and school outcomes* (National Bureau of Economic Policy Working Paper No. 17243). Retrieved from http://www.nber.org/papers/w17243.pdf

Borko, H. (2004, November). *Professional development and teachers learning: Mapping the terrain. Educational Researcher, 33*(8), 3–15.

Coggshall, J. G., Ott, A., Behrstock, E., & Lasagna, M. (2009). *Retaining teacher talent: The view from Generation Y.* New York: Public Agenda.

Csikszentmihalyi, M. (1990). *Flow: The psychology of optimal experience.* New York: Harper and Row.

Csikszentmihalyi, M. (1997). *Finding flow: The psychology of engagement with everyday life* New York: Harper and Row.

Danielson, C. (2013). *The framework for teaching evaluation instrument* (2013 ed.). Princeton, NJ: Danielson Group.

Darling-Hammond, L. (1998). Teacher learning that supports student learning. *Educational Leadership, 55*(5), 6–11.

Darling-Hammond, L. (2012). *Creating a comprehensive system for evaluating and supporting effective teaching.* Stanford, CA: Stanford Center for Opportunity Policy in Education.

Darling-Hammond, L. (2014). One piece of the whole: Teacher evaluation as a part of a comprehensive system for teaching and learning. *American Educator, 38*(1), 4–13.

Darling-Hammond, L., Wei, R. C., Andree, A., Richardson, N. & Orphanos, S. (2009). *School redesign network at Stanford University Professional Learning in the learning profession: A status report on teacher development in the U.S and abroad.* Dallas, TX: National Staff Development Council.

Davis, K. S. (2003). "Change is hard": What science teachers are telling us about reform and teacher learning of innovative practices. *Science Education, 87*(1), 3–30.

Easton, L. B. (Ed.). (2008). *Powerful designs for professional learning* (2nd ed.). Oxford, OH: National Staff Development Council.

Edmonson, A. C. (2012). *Teaming: How organizations learn, innovate, and compete in the knowledge economy.* San Francisco: Jossey-Bass.

Eisenbach, B. B. (2014, February). Words that encourage. *Education Leadership, 71*(5), 70–72.

Elmore, R. F. (2004). *School reform from the inside out: Policy, practice, and performance.* Cambridge, MA: Harvard Education Press.

Evaluation glossary. (n.d.). Western Michigan University, The Evaluation Center. Retrieved from http://www.wmich.edu/evalctr/

Fullan, M. (2014). *The principal: Three keys to maximizing impact.* San Francisco: Jossey-Bass.

Fuller, E., Baker, B., & Young, M. (2007). *The relationship between principal characteristics, school-level teacher quality and turnover, and student achievement* (*Working Paper Series, Federal Reserve Bank of Atlanta*). Retrieved from http://shankerblog.org/wp-content/uploads/2012/07/fullerbakeryoung_aera2007.pdf

Garet, M.S., Porter, A.C., Desimone, L., Birman, G. F., Yoon, K. S. (2001). What makes professional development effective? Results from a national sample of teachers. *American Educational Research Journal, 38*(4), 915–945.

Garmston, R. J., & Wellman, B. M. (2013). *The adaptive school: A sourcebook for developing collaborative groups* (2nd ed.). Lanham, MD: Rowan and Littlefield.

Gloor, P. A. (2006). *Swarm creativity.* Oxford: Oxford University Press.

Goddard, Y., Goddard, R., & Tschannen-Moran, M. (2007). A theoretical and empirical investigation of teacher collaboration for school improvement and student achievement in public elementary schools. *Teachers College Record, 109*(4), 877–896.

Guskey, T. R. (2000). *Evaluating professional development.* Thousand Oaks, CA: Corwin Press.

Guskey, T. R. (2002). Professional development and teacher change, *Teachers and Teaching: Theory and Practice, 8*(3), 381–391.

Hall, G. E., & Hord, S. M. (2015). *Implementing change: Patterns, principles, and potholes.* Princeton, NJ: Princeton.

Hargreaves, A. (2003). *Teaching in the knowledge society: Education in the age of insecurity.* New York: Teachers College Press.

Hargreaves, A., & Fullan, M. (2012). *Professional capital: Transforming teaching in every school.* New York: Teachers College Press.

Hiebert, J. Gallimore, R., & Stigler, J. W. A. (2002). Knowledge base for the teaching profession: What would it look like and how can we get one? *Educational Researcher, 31*(5), 3–15.

Hirsh, S., & Hord, S. H. (2012). *A playbook for professional learning: Putting the standards into action.* Oxford, OH: Learning Forward.

Hord, S. H. (2009). Professional learning communities. *JSD, 30*(1), 40–43.

Hord, S. H., Roussin, J. L., & Sommers, W. A. (2010). *Guiding professional learning communities.* Thousand Oaks, CA: Corwin.

Ingersoll, R., & Merril. L. (2010). Who's teaching our children? *Educational Leadership, 67*(8), 14–20.

Jordan, H. R., Mendro, R., & Weerasinghe, D. (1997). *Teacher effects on longitudinal student achievement: A preliminary report on research on teacher effectiveness.* Paper presented at the National Evaluation Institute, Indianapolis, IN.

Joyce, B., & Showers, B. (2002). *Student achievement through staff development* (3rd ed.). Alexandria, VA: Association for Supervision and Curriculum Development.

Learning Forward. (2012). *Standards for Professional Learning.* Oxford, OH: Author.

National Research Council. (2000). *How people learn: Brain, mind, experience, and school.* Washington, DC: National Academy Press.

Ontario Ministry of Education. (2010). Leading the instructional core: An interview with Richard Elmore. *In Conversations, 11*(3), 1–12.

Palomba, C. A., & Banta, T. W. (1999). *Assessment essentials: Planning, implementing, and improving assessment in higher education.* San Francisco: Jossey-Bass.

Reeves, D. B. (2010). *Leading change in your school: How to conquer myths, build commitment, and get results.* Alexandria, VA: Association for Supervision and Curriculum Development.

Scardamalia, M., & Bereiter, C. (2006). Knowledge building: Theory, pedagogy, and technology. In K. Sawyer (Ed.), *Cambridge handbook of the learning sciences* (pp. 97–118). New York: Cambridge University Press.

SEDL. (1997). Realizing school improvement through understanding the change process. *Issues About Change, 1*(1).

Skaalivick, E. M., & Skaalvick, S. (2010). Teacher self-efficacy and teacher burnout: A study of relations. *Teaching and Teacher Education, 26,* 1059–1069.

Standards for Professional Learning. (2012). Learning Forward.

Teaching Works. (n.d.). *High Leverage Practices,* University of Michigan. Retrieved from http://www.teachingworks.org/work-of-teaching/high-leverage-practices

U.S. Department of Education. (2014). Office of School Turnaround. Retrieved from http://www2.ed.gov/about/offices/list/oese/ost/index.html

Resources

Reflection on Learning Design Cycle 1

Participants:

Date:

Connection to Five Agreed-On Practices:

What was studied and planned?

What was implemented in the classroom?

What was learned from looking at student artifacts?

What changes need to be made for Cycle 2? What do you want to remember?

Reflection on Learning Design Cycle 2

Participants:

Date:

Connection to Five Agreed-On Practices:

What was studied and planned?

```


```

What was implemented in the classroom?

```


```

What was learned from looking at student artifacts?

```


```

What do you want to add to the Professional Knowledge Base?

Collaborative Planning, Teaching, and Assessing (CPTA)

Part 1—Planning	Part 2—Teaching	Part 3—Assessing
• Look at the objectives of the lesson • Align the objectives of the state standards • Study the standards • Identify learning targets for students • Plan the lesson flow • Look at the "Five Agreements" to identify intentional learning • Identify 1–3 research-based strategies to use during the lesson • Choose evidence of student understanding to bring to the "Assessment" session • Decide how each adult will participate during the lesson	• One teacher facilitates the collaboratively planned lesson • Teacher names the specific target or strategy used during the lesson so it is explicit to students • Observing teachers record student reactions and engagement with the intended strategy • Teacher stops class three minutes before the bell or end of lesson to give students the exit ticket • Teachers collect student work samples and exit tickets to bring to the "Assessment" session	• Teacher who taught the lesson shares first impressions of using intended strategies and overall observations of the lesson • Look at student work samples of exit tickets • Each teacher chooses an interesting strategy or way of thinking to share with the group • Identify students' misconceptions or misunderstandings • Identify strategies to support student growth as measured by the state standards • Reflect on CPTA as a learning design—what did you learn that you can apply in your class?

Checklist

1. How can your school implement the CPTA learning design?

2. When and where could teachers plan?

3. Who initiates, coordinates, and schedules the CPTA cycle?

4. Why would teachers select this learning design?

Peer Teaching

Part 1—Planning	Part 2—Teaching	Part 3—Assessing
• Look at the objectives of the lesson • Align the objectives to the state standards • Study the standards • Identify learning targets for students • Plan the lesson flow • Look at the "Five Agreements" to identify intentional learning • Identify 1–3 research-based strategies to use during the lesson • Choose evidence of student understanding to bring to the "Assessment" session • Decide how each teacher will participate during the lesson	• One or both teachers facilitate the collaboratively planned lesson • Teacher names the specific target or strategy used during the lesson so it is explicit to students • Observing teachers record student reactions and engagement with the intended strategy • Teacher stops class three minutes before the bell or end of lesson to give students the exit ticket • Teachers collect student work samples and exit tickets to bring to the "Assessment" session	• Teachers share first impressions of using intended strategies and overall observations of the lesson • Look at student work samples of exit tickets • Each teacher chooses an interesting strategy or way of thinking to share with the group • Identify students' misconceptions or misunderstandings • Identify strategies to support student growth as measured by the state standards • Reflect on Peer Teaching as a learning design— what did you learn that you can apply in your class?

Checklist

1. How can your school implement the Peer Teaching learning design?

2. When and where could teachers plan?

3. Who initiates, coordinates, and schedules the Peer Teaching cycle?

4. Why would teachers select this learning design?

Vertical Team Study

Part 1—Planning	Part 2—Teaching	Part 3—Assessing
• Identify the area of need for vertical learning • Identify the specific vertical learning focus • Set common goals using the "Five Agreements" to identify intentional learning • Identify resources, videos, research to study • Identify 1–3 research-based strategies to use during a lesson • Identify the "lesson flow" and where the strategies will be integrated in the lesson • Choose evidence of student understanding to bring to the "Assessment" session • Decide how each teacher will participate during the lesson	• One or more teachers facilitate the lesson • Teacher names the specific target or strategy used during the lesson so it is explicit to students • Observing teachers record student reactions and engagement with the intended strategy • Teachers collect student work samples and exit tickets to bring to the "Assessment" session	• Teachers share first impressions of using intended strategies and overall observations of the lesson • Look at student work samples, student observations, and anecdotes • Identify students' misconceptions or misunderstandings • Identify strategies to support student growth as measured by the state standards • Reflect on Vertical Team Study as a learning design—what did you learn that you can apply in your class?

Checklist

1. How can your school implement the Vertical Team learning design?

2. When and where could teachers plan?

3. Who initiates, coordinates, and schedules the Vertical Team cycle?

4. Why would teachers select this learning design?

Intentional Practicing With Student Response

Part 1—Planning	Part 2—Teaching	Part 3—Assessing
• Use data to determine need • Study effective instructional strategies • Decide which strategies to practice • Practice using the strategies with other teachers • Look at the "Five Agreements" to identify intentional learning • Design a lesson integrating the specific strategy • Choose evidence of student understanding to bring to the "Assessment" session • Decide how each teacher will participate during the lesson	• One or more teachers facilitate the collaboratively planned lesson • Teacher names the specific target or strategy used during the lesson so it is explicit to students • Teachers clearly states purpose for students using the strategy • Observing teachers record student reactions and engagement with the intended strategy • Teacher stops class three minutes before the bell or end of lesson to give students the exit ticket • Teachers collect student work samples and exit tickets to bring to the "Assessment" session	• Teachers share first impressions of using intended strategies and overall observations of the lesson • Look at student work samples of exit tickets • Each teacher chooses an interesting response for using the strategy • Identify students' misconceptions or misunderstandings • Identify strategies to support student growth as measured by the state standards • Reflect on Intentional Practicing with Student Response as a learning design—what did you learn that you can apply in your class?

Checklist

1. How can your school implement the Intentional Practice with Student Response learning design?

2. When and where could teachers plan?

3. Who initiates, coordinates, and schedules the Intentional Practice cycle?

4. Why would teachers select this learning design?

Using Technology

Part 1—Planning	Part 2—Teaching	Part 3—Assessing
• Identify the area of technology to use and clearly state the reason for using • Study how to use the technology • Design a lesson using or integrating technology • Align the objectives to the state standards • Study the standards • Identify learning targets for students • Look at the "Five Agreements" to identify intentional learning • Choose evidence of student understanding to bring to the "Assessment" session • Decide how each teacher will participate during the lesson	• One or more teachers facilitate the collaboratively planned lesson using or integrating technology • Teacher names the specific target or strategy used during the lesson so it is explicit to students • Observing teachers record student reactions and engagement with the intended strategy • Teacher stops class three minutes before the bell or end of lesson to give students the exit ticket • Teachers collect student work samples and exit tickets to bring to the "Assessment" session	• Teacher who facilitated shares first impressions of integrating or using technology and overall observations of the lesson • Look at student work samples of exit tickets • Each teacher chooses an interesting strategy or way of thinking to share with the group • Identify students' misconceptions or misunderstandings • Identify strategies to support student growth as measured by the state standards • Reflect on Using Technology as a learning design—what did you learn that you can apply in your class?

Checklist

1. How can your school implement the Using Technology learning design?

2. When and where could teachers plan?

3. Who initiates, coordinates, and schedules the Using Technology cycle?

4. Why would teachers select this learning design?

Studying Video With Application

Part 1—Planning	Part 2—Teaching	Part 3—Assessing
• Choose a video to study based on intended learning aligned to data and to the Five Agreements • Study the video and identify specific strategy to implement • Design a lesson integrating the using the video based strategy • Align the lesson to the state standards • Study the standards • Identify learning targets for students • Choose evidence of student understanding to bring to the "Assessment" session • Decide how each teacher will participate during the lesson	• One or more teachers facilitate the collaboratively planned lesson using integrating the strategy from video • Teacher names the specific target or strategy used during the lesson so it is explicit to students • Observing teachers record student reactions and engagement with the intended strategy • Teacher stops class three minutes before the bell or end of lesson to give students the exit ticket • Teachers collect student work samples and exit tickets to bring to the "Assessment" session	• Teacher who facilitated shares first impressions for integrating the strategy and overall observations of the lesson • Look at student work samples of exit tickets • Each teacher chooses an interesting strategy or way of thinking to share with the group • Identify students' misconceptions or misunderstandings • Identify strategies to support student growth as measured by the state standards • Reflect on Studying Video with Application as a learning design—what did you learn that you can apply in your class?

Checklist

1. How can your school implement the Studying Video with Application learning design?

2. When and where could teachers plan?

3. Who initiates, coordinates, and schedules the Studying Video cycle?

4. Why would teachers select this learning design?

Lesson Design

Part 1—Planning	Part 2—Teaching	Part 3—Assessing

• Identify a teaching problem based on student needs and establish an overarching goal
• Develop a research question
• Design a lesson to research
• Focus the lesson on student thinking, learning, and misunderstanding
 	
  o Build a context for the lesson
  o Identify learning targets and criteria for success
  o Engage students with concepts
  o Design a way for students to share their thinking
 	
• Identify evidence to collect to assess student learning of the target
	• Enact and observe the lesson
	• One teacher facilitates the lesson, the other teachers observe and document student thinking (NOTE: Teachers do not interact with the students)
	• Collect evidence of student thinking, such as work samples, pictures, videos, anecdotes, and student conversations
		• Debrief, reflect, and revise the lesson based on the data collected
		• Evaluate the lesson's impact on student learning
		• Share the results

Checklist

1. How can your school implement the Lesson Study learning design?

2. When and where could teachers plan?

3. Who initiates, coordinates, and schedules the Lesson Study cycle?

4. Why would teachers select this learning design?

Shared Learning With Teachers, Principals, and Coaches

Part 1—Planning	Part 2—Teaching	Part 3—Assessing
• Align the lesson to the state standards • Study the standards • Identify learning targets for students • Choose evidence of student understanding to bring to the "Assessment" session • Decide how each teacher, principal, and coach will participate during the lesson	• One or more teachers facilitate the collaboratively planned lesson using integrating the strategy from video • Teacher names the specific target or strategy used during the lesson so it is explicit to students • Observing teachers record student reactions and engagement with the intended strategy • Teacher stops class three minutes before the bell or end of lesson to give students the exit ticket • Teachers collect student work samples and exit tickets to bring to the "Assessment" session	• Teacher who facilitated shares first impressions for integrating the strategy and overall observations of the lesson • Look at student work samples of exit tickets • Each teacher chooses an interesting strategy or way of thinking to share with the group • Identify students' misconceptions or misunderstandings • Identify strategies to support student growth as measured by the state standards • Reflect on Studying Video with Application as a learning design— what did you learn that you can apply in your class?

Checklist

1. How can your school implement the Shared Learning design?

2. When and where could teachers plan?

3. Who initiates, coordinates, and schedules the Shared Learning cycle?

4. Why would teachers, coaches, and principals select this learning design?

Creative and Innovative Teaching

Part 1—Planning	Part 2—Teaching	Part 3—Assessing
• Identify the creative activity or innovation to try in the classroom • Pose questions and concerns about the innovation • Specify the intended results from using the creative activity or innovation • Study research about the creative activity or innovation • Design a classroom experience using the creative activity or innovation • Clarify roles during the experience • Align the experience to the state standards • Choose evidence of student understanding to bring to the "Assessment" session • Decide how each teacher will participate in the classroom	• One or more teachers facilitate the collaboratively planned classroom experience using the innovation • Observing teachers record student reactions and engagement with the intended innovation • Teachers collect student artifacts and exit tickets to bring to the "Assessment" session	• Teacher who facilitated shares first impressions for integrating the innovation • Look at student work samples of exit tickets • Identify outcomes of using the innovation • Reflect on Creative and Innovative Teaching as a learning design—what did you learn that you want to build on?

Checklist

1. How can your school implement the Creative and Innovative Teaching learning design?

2. When and where could teachers plan?

3. Who initiates, coordinates, and schedules the Creative Teaching cycle?

4. Why would teachers select this learning design?

Index

A SAGE Company

Corwin is committed to improving education for all learners by publishing books and other professional development resources for those serving the field of PreK–12 education. By providing practical, hands-on materials, Corwin continues to carry out the promise of its motto: **"Helping Educators Do Their Work Better."**

Advancing professional learning for student success

Learning Forward (formerly National Staff Development Council) is an international association of learning educators committed to one purpose in K–12 education: Every educator engages in effective professional learning every day so every student achieves.